Healthcare Money Campfire Stories

16 Lessons in the Business of Healing

Eric Bricker, MD

AHealthcareZ
2591 Dallas Parkway Suite 300
Frisco, TX 75034
www.AHealthcareZ.com

ISBN 9781703360714

First Edition

Dedication:

To Lauren

Contents

Healthcare Money Campfire Stories

Introduction

This book is a collection of brief stories. These stories were experienced by me personally. The stories are true, but the names of people and some organizations have been changed. The conversations are reproduced from my memory.

This book is intended for people who are change agents in healthcare, health insurance and employee benefits.

The reason for reading this book is to see that the role of money in healthcare has more implications than meet the eye.

Going forward, I hope you will see additional implications of money in healthcare more clearly.

Background

The mail had arrived. My welcome packet from college was by far the largest piece that day. I was accepted into the general College of Arts and Sciences at Northwestern University because I did not have a specific major in mind.

In the forms I had to fill out, there was a check box to indicate if I was 'Pre-Med.' The form said that if I was even thinking about being Pre-Med, then I should check the box so that a Pre-Med advisor could be assigned to me at the beginning of my freshman year. The forms said there was a lot of preparation that needed to start at the very beginning of college. I checked the box. That's how I became a doctor.

Well, there is a little more to it than that. Our family lived in the suburbs of Washington, D.C. The National Institutes of Health (NIH) were one town over. In school, I had always been interested in math and science. Our family attended church along with another family, where both the husband and wife were researchers at the NIH. They had a son who was in Sunday school with me. The wife knew I was interested in science and during my sophomore year of high school asked me if I wanted to apply for a summer internship in her lab at the NIH. It sounded interesting, but more importantly it was a job that paid and it was in air conditioning. My only summer job plans were mowing our lawn and the occasional neighbor's lawn.

The lab was run by a woman scientist. The woman from church reported to her. The PhD student who worked in the lab was a woman. The other summer intern was a woman from another local high school. I cannot say enough great things about the great mentoring and influence that these women had on me.

As one can imagine, the experience at the NIH opened my eyes to the amazing world of biological research. After that first summer and repeated summer internships in the same lab, I sat down with the director of our lab and told her that while the experience was 'cool' (I think that was the word I used), I could not imagine working in a lab for the rest of my life. The work was repetitive and slow. My own impatience was too much.

However, I still thought biology, human health and disease were fascinating. "Well then you might want to think about becoming a doctor," she counseled me. The thought had never crossed my mind. I'm not sure why. It was an interesting suggestion.

I attended undergrad in the 1990s. I majored in economics simply because I needed a back-up plan if I didn't get into medical school. The general opinion was that it was 'impossible' to get into medical school. I figured with an economics degree I could get a job. When my senior year came, I wanted to join the Peace Corps before going to medical school. I filled out the application, did the interview and figured I would be assigned to West Africa because I could speak a little French and the Peace Corps sent many volunteers there.

My acceptance packet came. It was not West Africa. I had been assigned to Eritrea—a country in East Africa between Ethiopia and the Red Sea. In fact, Eritrea was a very new country. It used to be a part of Ethiopia and had recently fought for its independence. Ethiopia wanted it back. There was still active fighting.

After some research regarding the war, I decided not to go.

Again, I had a 'Plan B' in case I was not accepted into the Peace Corps. I would get a job, take the MCAT—the entrance exam for medical school—and attend medical school in 2 years. I had interviewed on campus for two jobs and gone to a second round of interviews for both. They were healthcare consulting jobs. I received one rejection and one acceptance. I asked the company that had accepted me—Stockamp & Associates—if I could have until later in the spring to let them know my response. They agreed. After saying 'No' to the Peace Corps, I said 'Yes' to the healthcare consulting job and began work in August 1998.

I worked for two years as a hospital revenue cycle consultant. That is 'industry speak' for showing hospitals how to bill and collect payment from Medicare, Medicaid, commercial insurance carriers and patients themselves.

In the 1990s the internet was still new, so most hospital billing was done on paper. Hospital billing offices were frequently a mess—literally stacks and stacks of unsent bills and stacks and stacks of returned bills that had been denied payment for a myriad of reasons.

The hospital employees and management were doing the best they could, but the result was that many hospitals had 90 to 120 days' worth of unpaid bills. In business, these unpaid bills are called 'Accounts Receivable.' Stockamp almost exclusively worked at large academic medical centers, which would generate about one to three million dollars of bills a day. Therefore, 90 to 120 days' worth of bills equals accounts receivable of $90 million to $360 million. Having that much money in accounts receivable causes all sorts of cashflow problems for hospitals—some were even having trouble making payroll.

The hospitals where I worked were nationally and even internationally known—some of the best in the world. I learned a lot.

Just as importantly, I worked with amazing people at Stockamp. It was a company of about 100 employees that was founded by a handful of people that had left one of the largest consulting firms in the US. At Stockamp, I also worked with Scott Schoenvogel who would eventually become my business partner and CEO of the company that we founded—Compass Professional Health Services. Stockamp no longer exists. It was bought by and folded into Huron Consulting where many of the Stockamp leaders still work today.

I was living in Chicago at the time. Like many consultants I would fly to the client site on Monday morning, stay at a corporate apartment during the week, fly home on Thursday night and work remotely from my apartment on Friday. I would spend all day Saturday and Sunday studying for the MCAT and then later filling out applications for medical school.

Eventually, the medical school requests for interviews came. I interviewed at schools in New York City, California and Chicago. At one interview in New York my interviewer was a pathologist. We sat down and he said to me, "I see here on your application that you are from Illinois. Do they have a state medical school in Illinois?" I thought that was a funny question—of course Illinois has a medical school. "Yes," I responded.

He proceeded, "You should go there. This medical school is very expensive. The cheapest medical schools are the state medical schools. Your education will be the same. You can become whatever type of doctor you want. Go to the medical school in Illinois. Don't come here." "Is there anything I can say to change your mind?" I asked. "No." We stared at each other for an awkward moment. My interview ended.

I was disheartened to say the least. I had taken time off work to go to this interview. The flight had cost a lot of money. It was my first interview.

I went to a handful of other medical school interviews, including the University of Illinois at Chicago College of Medicine (UIC). I was accepted at UIC and enrolled. The pathologist was right.

The University of Illinois College of Medicine has several campuses across the state with the largest campus being in Chicago—where I attended. It is the largest medical school in the US, graduating about 400 new doctors every year.

Ironically, the school's own hospital is small—not the behemoth academic medical center that most medical schools have. As a result, the school sends its students to hospitals all over the Chicago area for clinical rotations: Cook County Hospital, the West Side VA, and community hospitals in both wealthy and poor parts of Chicago and its suburbs. This setup provides for great exposure to the diversity within the US Healthcare System—a setup that is unique among medical schools in the US. This benefit was just dumb luck for me, but it was the best possible experience to teach me about the variety of ways money impacts the practice of medicine.

During the third year of medical school, students rotate through the various specialties: surgery, pediatrics, Ob/Gyn, internal medicine, etc. My internal medicine rotation was at the VA. It convinced me to become a general internist. I loved the people. It was fun.

In my final year of medical school, I decided I wanted a career in healthcare policy research while on faculty at an academic medical center. It would be a path to help solve some of the problems I saw at Stockamp, while still seeing patients and teaching medical students. I loved medical school. I could be at a medical school for the rest of my career.

I applied to well-known hospitals for residency in San Francisco, Chicago, and Baltimore. I was accepted at Johns Hopkins Hospital in Baltimore. With its great reputation, proximity to Washington, D.C. and track record of working with the Centers for Medicare and Medicaid Services (CMS), it was a good fit given my interest in healthcare policy. Also, I was from Maryland originally and my family was there.

My intern year at Johns Hopkins was the worst year of my life. I would work at the hospital over 30 hours straight every fourth day and night. We had only four weekend days off a month. I was sleep deprived. The hospital pace was so fast that there was never time to eat. I was hungry. My fellow residents were great, but we had few days off at the same time. When they were off, I was working and vice versa. I was lonely. I became short tempered and bitter. I knew these were going to be the residency requirements, but knowing about them in theory and experiencing them are two different things.

My second and third years of residency were much better. I met my wife, Lauren. They say it's always darkest before the dawn and that was the case for me. I love her dearly. We have created a wonderful life together.

After my intern year I decided I did not want a career in academic medicine conducting healthcare policy research. During medical school I had kept in touch with Scott Schoenvogel from Stockamp. We had one lunch in Chicago when he was there on a work trip and I was in medical school. We had one phone call three years later when I asked him to help my roommate who was moving to Dallas, where Scott lived. We had briefly talked about what we could do to help people in healthcare as a business. In the fall of my second year of residency I called Scott and asked if he remembered our conversation. He had.

Many phone calls later and after Scott convinced his college roommate Cliff Sentell to join us, we formed the company Compass Professional Health Services.

Lauren and I married at the end of my residency. I found a part-time job at a hospital in a suburb of Dallas. Lauren and I bought a house one town over.

Compass was a healthcare navigation service for employer-sponsored health plans. We knew people needed help with all the administrative work in healthcare and health insurance. Doing so would not only improve their care and make things easier, but also save money.

Compass provided price-transparency, quality comparisons, prescription drug cost reduction, benefit plan explanation, open enrollment decision support, appointment scheduling and problem medical bill resolution. Compass was hired by employers to support their employees as part of their employee benefits package. That benefits package typically included health insurance, dental insurance, vision insurance, other types of benefits and... Compass. Employees and their family members interacted with our Compass healthcare navigation experts—called 'Health Pros'—by phone, email and smartphone app.

Historically, there was no administrative 'medical home' for people and Compass filled that void. For example, many times when a person had a problem medical bill, they would call their insurance company, be told it's not the insurance company's fault and need to contact the doctor. When the person then contacted the doctor's office, they were told it's not the doctor's fault and to call their insurance company. Now the person was stuck in the middle with no one to help.

Compass would step in, no matter what, act as the 'ombudsman' and advocate on behalf of the person to solve the problem. Compass did not make medical decisions—we did not want to 'play doctor.' However, Compass recommended doctors that met the person's specific needs. We then made sure their care was coordinated, administratively easy and billed accurately.

The trend in employee health insurance for the last 10 years has been Consumer Direct Health Plans (CDHPs) with a higher deductible and an associated Health Savings Account or Health Reimbursement

Arrangement. Traditional health insurance has little financial incentive for people or doctors to be good stewards of spending. The purpose of a CDHP was to change people's behavior to take care of their health better and be better consumers of the employer's healthcare spending and their own spending. If people were healthier and were less wasteful in using healthcare services, then they would keep more of their Health Savings Account money every year to use in the future. That was the theory. It's debatable as to whether it has borne out.

Compass was the necessary member-guidance tool to help employees with this new CDHP insurance plan. Compass grew to over 2,000 employer clients including Southwest Airlines, T-Mobile and Chili's Restaurants. Compass clients also included over 50 municipalities, major universities, manufacturers, banks, law firms, energy companies and healthcare organizations themselves. Yes, hospitals and physician practices would hire Compass to help their own employees navigate the complex healthcare system that they themselves created. I suppose that is the finest form of flattery. Across all those clients, Compass supported about two million people when you include the employees and their family members.

As the Chief Medical Officer of Compass, my responsibilities were in sales, marketing and account management. When cofounding a business, nothing happens until 'something gets sold,' as the expression goes—so I had to sell. With no previous experience in these areas, it was a crash-course in self-education and a lot of trial-and-error. I would cold-call insurance brokers and HR managers. I'm probably one of the few physicians in America who cold calls.

I created a lead generation list of over 10,000 contacts, which I and a small team turned into leads for our sales team. I personally sold to insurance brokers, HR and CFOs weekly for 11 years. I wrote a weekly blog for 10 years that eventually grew to 30,000 pageviews a month. We created a monthly educational webinar series that had upwards of 200 attendees per month. We created and trained an account management team to foster the success of our 2,000 clients. I would negotiate contracts. It was an amazing front-row seat to business and employer-sponsored healthcare in America.

My responsibilities also included the clinical design of our service and its ongoing development. Compass could anticipate the specific administrative, quality and cost challenges for patients given their medical situation. The administrative challenges for an expectant mother versus a person with a chronic disease like diabetes are very different. Likewise, the quality and cost issues for a person anticipating spine surgery versus a person needing a treatment facility for a drug addiction are also very different. Compass tailored its 'non-medical' healthcare support based on a patient's medical needs. It was exactly what people needed.

Of course, I did none of these efforts alone. Scott Schoenvogel, Cliff Sentell and our Compass executives, managers and employees worked together as a team. Our Compass people worked hard, were smart and most importantly, were beyond trustworthy. Even better, they were amazingly kind and pleasant. We grew to 300 employees. Compass was eight parts joy, two parts work.

Compass was then purchased by Alight Solutions in the Summer of 2018. Alight is a 10,000-employee company that was created in 2017 when it separated from the international insurance giant Aon. Alight is the former benefits administration and human resources outsourcing business unit of Aon and was sold to the private equity firm, The Blackstone Group. I left Compass and Alight in November 2018.

I love spending time with my family and have been able to do so more since then. I also saw an opportunity to teach others what I had learned as a combined 'hospital-finance-consultant-doctor-salesman-entrepreneur.' I had seen a lot. I wanted to share what I had learned.

I started a healthcare finance video journal called AHealthcareZ. AHealthcareZ posts brief educational videos five days per week. The topics range from explaining how hospitals and insurance companies negotiate their prices to how pharmacy benefit managers make money to how medical coding works. The videos are uploaded to the AHealthcareZ.com website, emailed to a list of subscribers and posted on LinkedIn. I chose LinkedIn since healthcare finance is mostly a business-to-business matter and LinkedIn is the top social media platform for business-to-business related issues.

The positive response has been more than I could have imagined. As of September 2019, AHealthcareZ has 80,000 video views per month across all platforms. Subscribers and commenters include insurance brokers, benefits consultants, hospital administrators, surgeons, primary care physicians, insurance carrier executives, drug company employees, human resources and employee benefits leaders, nurses, pharmacists, physical therapists... even university professors. Interestingly, there are many international viewers as well, many of whom are computer programmers in India that make software used in the US healthcare system.

My background has allowed me to see budgets being made, deals being negotiated and patients' being healed—or not. Healthcare and the role of money are not confusing. They make complete sense once you see the healthcare system from end-to-end. Let me tell you some true stories and let's learn together.

1

The R.O.A.D. to Happiness

"I want to be a Radiologist," said Bruno. He was one of my fellow first-year medical students. We were in medical school orientation. It was August of 2000. Our entering class of about 200 people sat at circular tables in a giant conference hall in our medical school's student union building. While sitting at the tables, we would listen to various speakers: The Dean, a senior cardiologist, the Head of Student Affairs, etc. In between sessions, there was time for chatting.

The subject of break-time chat was frequently what type of doctor each student wanted to be. Having no one in my family in medicine, I did not know that the type of doctor that you were had profound impacts on your lifestyle. I was naïve.

Having the most desirable lifestyle as a doctor meant: (1) a high income, (2) fewer overall hours of work, (3) less work on weekends and holidays and (4) less time being on call overnight with a pager. It was not so much 'what' you were doing, as much as how to get paid the most for the least amount of time. Bruno proceeded to educate me.

To maximize these four characteristics of lifestyle, the specialties of Radiology, Ophthalmology, Anesthesiology and Dermatology were at the top. They provided the most income for the least amount of work, weekends and overnight call. They formed the acronym R.O.A.D. and were known as the 'R.O.A.D. to Happiness.'

The next tier down included Orthopedic Surgery, ENT, Urology, Neurosurgery, Cardiology, Gastroenterology, General Surgery and the other Surgical Subspecialties. These were the 'proceduralist' specialties in that the doctors performed a lot of procedures that tended to be well compensated. These doctors made a lot of money, but they had to work a lot of hours, including overnight, weekends and holidays.

The next tier down were all the other internal medicine specialties such as Nephrology, Oncology and Endocrinology. Also included in this tier were other specialties such as Ob/Gyn, Emergency Medicine and Pathology. These specialties did not have as much money as the proceduralists.

The bottom tier were Pediatrics, General Internal Medicine, Family Practice and Psychiatry... in other words, primary care and mental health. These specialties had almost no procedures and dealt a lot with talking to patients, which takes a long time. Talking means less visits per day and less money.

Their patients were mostly on Medicare or Medicaid, as well. Medicare and Medicaid tend to reimburse doctors less than commercial insurance. So not only did these bottom tier doctors see fewer patients, but they were also paid less per patient, too. With that final comment, Bruno was done with his explanation.

I looked around the table at the other new medical students who were listening. They all nodded in agreement. "How do you know all this?!" I asked. "My dad's a cardiologist." "My mom's an oncologist." "Everyone knows this."

Ahh ha! Now I was getting it. The lifestyle implications of each specialty were passed on from parent doctor to child doctor. That's understandable since these children had to grow up in a household with a physician and saw firsthand the impact of their parents' chosen specialties on their families.

This hierarchy of physician specialties has some unintended consequences on the practice of medicine itself. The most desirable, tier-one specialties had the most competitive residencies. Therefore, the smartest students in medical school at the top of their class entered these areas. Tier two then had the next smartest batch of people. Tier three had the next cohort. Tier four had what was left.

Of course, it's more complicated than that. To become a cardiologist or gastroenterologist, one must do a residency in internal medicine first and then additional training in a specific cardiology or gastroenterology fellowship. Accordingly, there were tier two level medical students who applied to internal medicine residencies (which are tier four) as part of the required progression to become specialists.

Also, some incredibly bright medical students may have a 'calling' to work with children and so become pediatricians even though they could have been dermatologists. Every medical student knows this.

As a result of this hierarchy, the perception within the practicing physician community is that, tier four doctors are not as smart as the higher tiers. Tiers one, two and three tend to look down on tier four clinically, which means their judgement as a specialist regarding a patient supersedes that of the primary care physician. They will probably not admit this. They may not even believe it themselves, but it still subconsciously impacts their medical decision making.

This hierarchy is a problem because the higher tier specialists do not deal with the entire person. They only address one organ or part of the body—sometimes at the expense of other parts of the body. Helping the heart can hurt the kidneys. Taking a patient to orthopedic surgery can risk damage to the brain under anesthesia. A person may be in pain because they are depressed and no amount of surgery is going to help their depression. It's the tier four primary care and mental health doctors that typically think about the patient holistically—the very same doctors who are at the bottom of the doctor food chain.

Again, of course there are exceptions. There are holistically thinking cardiologists and orthopedic surgeons. However, they are the exception rather than the rule in my opinion.

Lesson Learned:

A potential component behind the over-testing, over-diagnosis and over-treatment of patients in America is the specialist-driven hierarchy among doctors. The 'do-more' specialties are on top. Somewhat obscurely, it is a hierarchy of intelligence rooted in money and lifestyle.

2

This Is All Fluid

During my third year of medical school, my first clinical rotation was general internal medicine at the West Side VA in Chicago. The rotation was three months in total—one month of outpatient clinic and two months of inpatient hospital wards.

As part of the outpatient clinic portion, medical students were to go on house calls with a VA nurse and medical assistant as part of a homecare program. As one can imagine, the program was intended to reach veterans who for various reasons could not make it to the outpatient clinic at the hospital. Lack of mobility was the most common reason.

I met with the nurse and assistant at the hospital and the three of us got into a teal Ford Taurus with the letters 'VA' painted on the two front doors. We then drove about 45 minutes south to visit a patient who had hypertension, diabetes and congestive heart failure (CHF).

He had been discharged from the hospital about one month ago for what is called a 'CHF Exacerbation.' In brief, his heart was not pumping strong enough to move the same amount of blood out as was returning. As a result, the veins become 'backed-up' and pressure builds in the microscopic capillaries—the smallest branches of the circulatory system. Eventually, the 'exacerbation' occurs when the fluid part of the blood—not the red blood cells—is pushed out of the blood stream because of the increased pressure into the tissues of the body. There is excess fluid in the lungs making it hard to breath and excess fluid in the legs making it hard to walk or even stand. To treat the CHF exacerbation, the patient is given intravenous (IV) diuretic medication that causes the kidneys to filter out the excess fluid, which the patient then urinates out of their body. Days or weeks later, enough fluid has been removed so that the patient can be switched to pill diuretic medications and discharged from the hospital.

Our Ford Taurus arrived at a collection of two-story, row houses. They were across the street from a field of overgrown grass that was filled with trash. Each row house had a small front yard with patches of dirt mixed with overgrown grass—all full of litter, too. Some of the windows were covered with plywood. A thin dog trotted across the parking lot. It was a poor part of town.

We walked up to the door. The medical assistant knocked. The nurse and I were behind her. A short, thin woman in jeans and an untucked flannel shirt opened the door. She did not make eye contact, turned and walked back into the house. She did not say anything. No hello. No 'who are you?' The medical assistant and nurse followed her. So did I, reluctantly.

The front door led directly to what looked like a family room. There was brown wood paneling on the walls, two light-brown, torn and stained sofas, a coffee table covered with several plates with half eaten food on them, paper towels, an ash tray and an old TV playing a daytime show. It was dim. Curtains were drawn over the front window. It smelled musty and of body odor. The woman who let us in had not said a word.

She continued through the family room to the back door. The room was small but extended the depth of the home from front-to-back. There was a storm door out the back with a picture window next to it with bars on the outside. She walked out the storm door and was no longer visible. The sun was in the East on the backside of the house. My eyes had started to adjust to the darkness of the home so that it seemed even brighter outside than normal.

Immediately to our left while facing the back door was a narrow staircase up to the second floor with brown, worn carpeting. "I'm coming," we heard the raspy voice of a middle-aged man coming from upstairs. We turned and faced up the staircase, waiting to see the man behind the voice.

First, we just saw the feet—bare, swollen and massive. Next we saw the legs, then midsection and arms as he steadied himself with the wooden railing. It shook every time he grabbed it. He was wearing grey sweatpants that had been cut into shorts. He had no shirt. He walked down sideways with his left foot stepping one step down and his right foot then following to the same step. He was the most obese person I had ever seen—we soon came to find out he weighed over 900 pounds.

He reached the bottom. We said hello. "Thank you for coming," he replied. He said his name was Maurice. "Come on upstairs."

After watching him precariously come down the stairs I said to myself there was no way he was going to make it back up. But he did, breathing heavily. The medical assistant followed, then the nurse, then me.

The staircase led directly into a bedroom that faced the front of the house. It had an oversized, old metal hospital bed, mattress, no sheets and a balled-up, cream-colored comforter pushed to the side. There was a small wooden dresser, more wood paneling on the walls, a brownish light fixture overhead and trash everywhere. The entire home was in squalor.

He sat on the edge of the bed. The nurse and medical assistant asked him how he was doing and begin to question him regarding his recent hospitalization, discharge and care at home. On the day Maurice went to the hospital, he had suddenly been unable to breath and called 911. He was so large that the ambulance crew could not lift him into the vehicle. They had to call the police and another ambulance crew to help. He said eventually about a dozen people were able to get him into the ambulance, which then drove him to the West Side VA.

Maurice paused. The nurse tried to check his blood pressure, but the cuff would not even come close to fitting around his arm. She stopped trying. He had a pannus—fat hanging off the front of the body—that was about the size of a kitchen table for four. They pricked

22

his finger to check his blood sugar. It read 132 on the glucometer. A little high, but not bad.

We continued to talk. Maurice was born and raised in Chicago. At 18 he was drafted into the Army and sent to the Vietnam War. He pulled out a small picture frame with a photo of him at 18 in a suit and tie with a woman in a wedding dress. It was his wedding photo. In the picture he was handsome, smiling, a little over 6 feet tall and thin. A picture of perfect health.

After serving in Vietnam, he married this woman from his neighborhood. The marriage lasted about a year. He said he saw things in Vietnam you couldn't imagine. He turned to drugs and alcohol to help him forget. His wife left him. He became very depressed and he ate.

Maurice then remarried and divorced two more times and is now married to his fourth wife—the woman who let us in. They have been married for two years. He received a check every month from the Army and he knew that was why she married him.

He no longer drank or did drugs. He had even lost 100 pounds, he said, by eating a strict die of only vegetables and soup. In other words, he used to be over 1,000 pounds. He said he knew because of the scale in the bed at the VA hospital. He was in the hospital about a year ago and it measured over 1,000 then. On his most recent trip, it measured in the 900s, according to him. "This is all fluid," Maurice explained. It was not all fluid. It was mostly fat.

"What do you do with yourself?" the nurse asked. He pointed to an old, open, black suitcase lying on the floor. It was filled with neatly arranged rows of hand-labeled cassette tapes. "I make mix tapes," Maurice replied. On the dresser there was a dual cassette-deck boom box. He listened to the radio and recorded songs that he liked. He also recorded from tape-to-tape. His face had been expressionless the whole time, but his voice brightened a little. "I've got some real good ones in there."

We examined Maurice. He lied on his side on the bed. The medical assistant and I pulled back his pannus as far as we could—it probably weighed over 100 pounds itself. The nurse checked the skin underneath and found it moist and raw from a yeast infection—a common problem in the skin folds of very obese people. She applied some anti-fungal powder to the best of her ability. "We'll leave the powder here. Do you have anyone to help you do this?" she asked. "No," Maurice answered.

After more questions and more examination, we wrapped up our house call. The nurse told Maurice to have less soup and to switch to the low-sodium kind. All the salt in the soup he ate probably caused his CHF exacerbation. Maurice was trying to do the right thing in losing weight. He had no idea that the soup had complicated his heart problem.

"Are you depressed, Maurice?" the nurse asked him. "Yes," Maurice answered. He was not taking any antidepressant medication and had not seen a psychiatrist in over a decade.

"Would you like help with your depression?" continued the nurse. "No. It's no use," he replied. The nurse asked Maurice if he would consider seeing a counselor. He said he would think about it.

The nurse told him the VA would come out and see him again in another month. We turned to leave and walked past Maurice's wife who had just come upstairs. Again, she said nothing, did not make any eye contact with us or Maurice, walked into the back bedroom and shut the door.

<u>Lesson Learned</u>:

If our thoughts are ill, our bodies will follow. If our families are ill, our bodies will likely follow too. No amount of care, medicine, money or 'healthcare system change' will heal our bodies unless we begin to heal our thoughts and our families.

3

The Second Time I've Been Attacked

During the third year of medical school, students do required rotations lasting from one to three months in the major specialties of doctoring: internal medicine, surgery, pediatrics, Ob/Gyn, etc. Psychiatry is one of these rotations.

I was fortunate at the University of Illinois College of Medicine. I was able to have first pick of where I did each of my third-year rotations. I had this priority because I did an independent research project while in medical school.

As previously mentioned, the University of Illinois College of Medicine sent its students all over Chicago for the different rotations. Locations varied from the main University Hospital, to the famous Cook County Hospital, to the West Side VA, to various community hospitals throughout the city and suburbs. Each of these hospitals was known for having particularly good rotations in certain specialties, largely based on the quality of teaching from the attending physicians.

For psychiatry, Illinois Medical Center was known as the best hospital because of the one doctor who ran the entire medical student rotation: Dr. S. Dr. S was a foreign born and foreign trained psychiatrist who did subsequent training after coming to the United States.

He was in his late 50s and had been a practicing psychiatrist in America for 30 years. He was even active in both local and national politics.

Dr. S was kind, soft spoken and exceedingly patient. He was everything you would expect in a psychiatrist. He wore brown slacks, a suit jacket, dress shirt and no tie. Often, he would accessorize his outfit with a silk, paisley neck scarf, like something out of a late 1960s movie. He had graying brown hair that was thinning on top, which he styled with a combover. He had a mustache. He looked how an 'old-school' psychiatrist would look. All he needed was a pipe.

Our month-long rotation at Illinois Medical Center had three students: Cathy, Ellen and me. On our first morning, we arrived in the lobby of the hospital, as instructed, and waited for the secretary from the Psychiatry Department to meet us. After approaching us and introducing herself, she took us up the elevator to the Inpatient Psychiatry Unit. Psychiatry Units are unique in hospitals in that they are locked. There are cameras on both sides of the entry door with monitors at the nurse's station for the clerk to watch. Our secretary escort pushed the intercom button and asked to be 'buzzed' in. "The new medical students are here for Dr. S," she said.

We heard the door buzz. Our escort pushed it open and we walked in. I was not sure what to expect, but it looked like a regular hospital floor. There was no one in the hallway and we took an immediate right and walked down a corridor, past about four patient rooms to the nurse's station.

Unlike most nurse's stations which were open to the hospital hallway, this nurse's station was enclosed in glass to the ceiling and had a locked door as well. Within the glass, you could see the 'chicken-wire' pattern of metal meant to reinforce the glass and prevent it from shattering. The reason for the 'shatter-proof' glass and locked door was to prevent any of the patients from forcefully entering the nurse's station.

The head nurse—referred to as the 'Charge Nurse'—informed us that Dr. S was seeing patients across the street at his office in the morning and would be over at the hospital in the afternoon. She recommended we go to a small instruction/family meeting room and read our psychiatry rotation textbook—so we did.

The morning was uneventful. We sat and read and engaged in occasional small talk. Nurses, techs and patients would walk past the open door to the room where we were. Rather than the usual hospital gowns that tied in the back, all the patients wore what looked like sky-blue pajamas. There was an indoor smoking room where the patients took smoke breaks. The room had similar shatter-proof glass and was small—about 8 feet by 10 feet. There were scheduled smoke breaks when about 15 people would cram into this small room. They were given about 10 minutes. Many of the patients on the floor had schizophrenia and people with this condition typically smoke—a lot. In the amount of time they were given for their smoke break, each patient could easily smoke multiple cigarettes. It was amazing to see the smoking room become incredibly hazy with the smoke of 30 plus cigarettes in a 10-minute period-of-time. Then they would all shuffle out and walk back to their rooms. The smoke would stay thick in the room for a long time. I was later told there was a vent that eventually cleared out the smoky air.

We went down to the hospital cafeteria for lunch and then returned to the psychiatry unit. We were buzzed in, walked down to the nurse's station and were buzzed in there as well. The Charge Nurse informed us that Dr. S was on the floor seeing a patient and to wait here and he would meet us when he had finished. We waited about five minutes.

Suddenly, there was shouting coming from the hallway near the locked entrance to the psychiatry unit. The shouting was one man's voice only. It was mostly unintelligible. We saw three male nurses through the shatter-proof glass of the nurse's station run in the direction of the shouting. They were each about six feet tall. Two small techs quickly rushed to the outside of the door to the nurse's station. We heard a buzz and then they entered. My fellow medical students and I looked at each other with an expression of alarm and confusion on our faces. We did not move.

"Call security," the Charge Nurse exclaimed to the clerk at the phone. The shouting continued. Again, only the one man's voice was heard. However, this time there was the sound of a struggle and the chirping of rubber-soled shoes on the tile floor—like during a basketball game.

Less than a minute later, a man ran to the door of the nurse's station and was immediately buzzed in. He almost dove into one of the rolling office-chairs. The chair rolled a couple of feet from his momentum. It was an older gentleman, brown pants, brown suit jacket, graying black hair styled in a combover that had been tussled and was sticking up and flopped over in the wrong direction so that it looked like the crest of a rooster. It was Dr. S. His eyes were wide and you could see the white fully around his dark iris and pupils. "This is only the second time I've been attacked in 25 years," he said—still breathless from his sprint down the hall.

Eventually the shouting stopped. The clerk picked up the phone. We had been cleared to leave the nurse's station. Dr. S did not introduce himself and neither did we, but it was obvious that we were his new medical students for the month. He said it would be a good idea if we just went home for the day and he would meet us back in the unit the next morning.

As we walked down the hall, we passed by a patient room that had the three male nurses we had seen run by the nurse's station. Four security guards in their navy blue, police-looking uniforms were there, too. They were standing around a bed with a man lying flat on his back with both arms and both legs in restraints at the head and foot of the bed. His eyes were closed. He was not moving. He was breathing calmly, but rapidly. I could see one of the nurses going to dispose of a needle and syringe. It turned out the nurse had just given the man who had attacked Dr. S an injection of a sedative. We left.

As soon as the door closed behind us to the Psychiatry Unity, Ellen exclaimed, "Holy crap! What was that?!" "I have no idea," I replied. "I don't know that I want to come back tomorrow," Ellen said.

The next day, Dr. S was all smiles and a mark of civility and equanimity. He explained that the man who had attacked him was one of his patients with schizophrenia who, in a fit of psychosis, struck him and tackled him to the ground. Dr. S then told us the story of when he had been attacked by a patient for the first time, 25 years earlier. It was in the psychiatry unit of a VA hospital also in Chicago. He apologized for us having had that event happen on our first day.

The next month was an amazing experience. Probably 80 percent of the patients on the floor had schizophrenia and were either a danger to themselves or to others. Another 10 percent were people with depression who were either suicidal or had psychotic features that made them dangerous. The remaining 10 percent were people with bipolar disorder who were having a manic episode and they were dangerous to either themselves or others as well.

Dr. S even had one patient with such prolonged and severe depression that he was almost catatonic. The patient ate very little. He would not get out of bed. He typically refused to talk and if he did, it was only one or two-word answers. He was middle aged, well over six feet tall and gaunt. Dr. S said the patient was a doctor himself who had gone to a medical conference in another city and upon his return, fell into his current depressed state.

After being in the hospital for several months and having many different medication regiments, Dr. S said he needed to try a different approach. He wanted to have electroconvulsive therapy (ECT) performed on the gentleman. Just like it sounds, ECT involves hooking electrodes up to a patient and shocking them so that it causes them to have a seizure. In theory, the seizure would 'snap them out' of their depression. ECT was used more frequently in the past, and Dr. S had seen it be successful with other patients.

The hospital where we were did not have a machine for ECT, so Dr. S arranged for the patient to be moved to another hospital about one mile away. The patient would then come back the same day.

In the procedure room at this other hospital, an anesthesiologist had attached monitors and the electrodes to the patient. The patient was unconscious. Dr. S flipped a switch on the ECT machine and turned a small, red dial.

The anesthesiologist had a blood pressure cuff around the arm of the patient. He had given the patient a paralytic medication through his IV so that he would not move and fall off the gurney when he had the seizure. However, he had intentionally fully inflated the blood pressure cuff so that blood was temporarily not flowing to the patient's left forearm and hand. Because blood was not flowing to the hand, the paralytic medication was not delivered to those muscles and therefore, his hand was not paralyzed. We could see his hand rapidly twitch from the seizure he was having in his brain. The seizure only lasted several seconds. That was it. We left.

When I saw the patient the next day, he was the same. Dr. S was not pleased, but he said it could take some time for the potential therapeutic effect of the ECT to occur.

The rotation concluded. We soon took the psychiatry test that all students take after completing their month-long rotation. I received almost a perfect score. I write this not as a reflection on myself, but rather as a reflection of the instruction by Dr. S. He was so detailed, thorough and kind. It was impossible not to learn. Cathy and Ellen also received exceedingly high scores.

Several months later, it was the end of my third year of medical school. I had come to find out from speaking with other students that my rotation with Dr. S was his second to last for the entire medical school. The hospital administration had shut down the medical student training program in psychiatry because they wanted Dr. S to spend all his time with patients and not with medical students. Supposedly, Dr. S had told the last group of students that the hospital was under new ownership and that the new owners needed him to bill more.

Lesson Learned:

Financial decisions at a hospital impact medical training. Educating future doctors is a money-losing proposition. If monetary goals are given top priority, short-term economic gain could come at the long-term cost of decreased medical student experiences and training.

Dr. S and dozens of my attending physicians had sacrificed countless hours teaching me instead of seeing more patients that they could bill. My tuition could not have made up the difference in revenue. They did a noble service and I am grateful.

Dr. T

During the fourth year of medical school, it is common for students to do 'visiting rotations' at academic medical centers other than their own. These visiting rotations are often used as an opportunity for a fourth-year student to see if the medical center is one where they would like to apply for residency. Given my interest in healthcare policy and being from the Washington, D.C. area originally, I did visiting rotations at both Georgetown University and George Washington University—more commonly referred to as just 'GW.'

Medical students can choose a specific area for their visiting rotation and I chose infectious diseases at GW. Each rotation was a month long and I had scheduled both rotations in D.C. back-to-back. I packed up my car and drove from Chicago to D.C.

At GW, we had a team of six for our infectious disease rotation: two fourth-year medical students, one internal medicine resident, two infectious disease fellows and one infectious disease attending physician. Our attending physician was Dr. T. Dr. T was a Filipino-American woman in her 60s. She had shoulder length black hair, deep lines of experience on her face and a countenance that went from very serious to smiling to very serious again, all within a second. It's like she would allow herself a moment of joy... and then get back to work. She shuffled as she walked. She wore a long white doctor's coat over a floral print dress.

Dr. T had been born and raised in the Philippines. She had attended medical school there as well. She had come to the United States decades ago and had been practicing medicine at GW ever since. She had even been the head of the Infectious Disease Division for a time before passing the position to another doctor.

Our infectious disease team would see patients in the hospital as requested by the other services—surgery, the ICU, the general medicine floor, etc. We would evaluate the patients, examine lab reports, even go to the microbiology lab to look at specimens under the microscope to identify bacteria or parasites. We would then recommend an antibiotic regimen and monitor the patient's progress on the IV medication.

It was a busy, fast-paced month. The mornings were early and the days were long. Dr. T spoke quickly and intensely. She was both stern and warm. She would correct us sharply but end her 'feedback' with a smile. She knew many of the nurses on the floor by name, which was unusual. Most attending physicians do not know the nurses' names. All the nurses knew who Dr. T was. She knew all the other attendings as well. They would give a brief wave and say hello to her by name everywhere in the hospital: in the ICU, in pathology to look at slides, in radiology to look at films.

This degree of familiarity with a physician at a large academic medical center is somewhat rare. There are hundreds of attending physicians. So much of the communication is run through the residents and the fellows, that the attendings rarely talk to each other and if they do, they often have never met or are mere acquaintances. But not Dr. T. You could tell she was somewhat the matron of the hospital.

As we approached the end of our month together, Dr. T said she was going to take us all out to a fancy Indian cuisine restaurant for lunch. This event was often a tradition at teaching hospitals: the attending physician would take their team out for either lunch or dinner at the end of working together for the month. This happened at my medical school and at Johns Hopkins Hospital where I did residency, too.

The restaurant was only a short walk from the hospital. We sat at a table outside on a second-floor, covered patio. It was a beautifully sunny day, cooler and with low humidity after the previous night's rain. We ordered. We asked Dr. T more about her story and her personal life. It turned out she lived close to where my grandparents did in a Maryland suburb of D.C.

It occurred to me that Dr. T had been working at GW for so long that she was probably there in the early 1980s. GW Hospital is famous for being the place where the Secret Service took President Ronald Reagan after he was shot by John Hinkley in March of 1981—only two months after he had been inaugurated.

"Were you there?" I asked. "Yes," Dr. T answered. "Did you see the Secret Service in the hospital?" I pressed. "Yes," she answered again. She continued, "President Reagan was one of my patients. I was part of the group of doctors that took care of him after he had been shot."

Wow! Dr. T had been a part of history! We had worked together the whole month and it had never come up and she had never mentioned it. In fact, GW is the closest hospital to the White House and I had noticed several of the doctors had pins on their white coats to signify that they were part of the special group that would take care of the President should he come to the hospital.

Had Dr. T and the doctors, nurses and staff at GW not saved President Reagan, we would have had George H. W. Bush as president much sooner. President Reagan would have been President for only about 60 days. It was the last time a President had been shot.

I asked Dr. T more questions, but she said, "We have talked enough about that." I knew to stop asking.

We concluded lunch and in a few days, we ended our month-long rotation together. President Reagan was one lucky guy to have Dr. T has his physician.

Lesson Learned:

Foreign born and foreign trained doctors, nurses and medical staff are some of the unsung heroes of our healthcare system. We literally could not survive without them.

There is an economic reason why the US has so many foreign healthcare workers. The labor market for healthcare is subject to supply and demand like other areas of the economy. There is greater demand for healthcare professionals than there is supply within the US. The reasons for this shortage are government regulation, insufficiently skilled Americans and lack of interest by workers in the US. The pay is good, but the hours are bad and the work itself can be unpleasant. Our country alone does not produce enough people to take care of all the unwell Americans—including the President.

5

Sweet Jesus

Mrs. B was a woman in her late 60s who had come to the Johns Hopkins Emergency Department after being discharged from a hospital in Washington, D.C. two days prior. She had been having worsening abdominal pain, nausea and vomiting. A CT scan at the hospital in D.C. had been read as 'pancreatitis'—inflammation of the pancreas. Mrs. B was admitted there for IV fluids and pain medication. After several days, she tried to eat some broth and could keep it down. She was discharged home. This is typical treatment for pancreatitis.

Once home, her abdominal pain, nausea and vomiting returned. Rather than take her back to the same hospital, her grown daughter decided to drive her up I-95 70 minutes to John Hopkins Hospital in Baltimore. Upon examination in the ER, another CT scan was ordered and this time it was not read as 'pancreatitis,' but rather as 'pancreatic mass, possible cancer.'

She was admitted to me from the ER on the third month of my intern year for further diagnostic workup, IV fluids and pain control. The gastroenterology (GI) doctors were called to evaluate Mrs. B for possible endoscopy and biopsy of the mass—a definitive diagnosis of pancreatic cancer could only be made with a biopsy. It took a day for the GI doctors to see her and she was put on the schedule for an endoscopy and biopsy in a couple days.

I would examine Mrs. B every morning around 6 AM and see her again on rounds with the internal medicine team around 11 AM. I would see her a third or even a fourth time during the afternoon and evening before I admitted new patients while on call in the hospital, went to my outpatient clinic to see patients in the afternoon or went home.

There are many slang terms and idioms in the hospital. Mrs. B had the 'positive nice person sign' for cancer--the origin of the expression being that it is frequently the nicest people that end up with cancer. You could tell Mrs. B was a wonderful person because her middle-aged daughter was kind as well. She would smile at me and say, "You're pretty good for a rookie." Mrs. B's kindness had been passed on to the next generation.

Several days into her hospitalization her heart rate suddenly jumped to about 120 beats per minute—up from about 70. The ECG showed normal heart electrical activity—but a rapid rate—which is called 'sinus tachycardia.' I took the ECG printout to my Senior Resident who was sitting with our Attending Physician. I addressed the Senior Resident and not the Attending Physician, as we were taught to follow the 'chain of command.'

"I think she has a PE," I said. PE stands for Pulmonary Embolism—a blood clot in the vessels of the lungs. It often causes chest pain and shortness of breath, but it also causes sinus tachycardia. In fact, sometimes the only thing a PE causes is sinus tachycardia and nothing else. A PE originates as a blood clot in the legs, which then breaks free, travels back to the heart and becomes suck in the lungs when the blood is pumped there to be oxygenated.

"Well if you think she has a PE, send her for a CT," said the Senior Resident. A CT scan of the chest is the standard test to diagnose a PE.

Very little happens as fast as you would like as an intern. By the time Mrs. B had gone for her CT, I needed to leave the hospital for the outpatient clinic about two miles away. While walking in the parking garage to my car, I received a page from radiology. I called back on my cell phone. "Your patient Mrs. B has a PE. It's big." I hung up, paged the intern who was covering for me in the hospital and told her the results and to start Mrs. B on a heparin drip—the blood thinner treatment for a PE. I paged the Senior Resident as well to let him know.

The next day when I returned to the hospital, Mrs. B was in a different room because she needed to be on a cardiac monitor. Her heart rate was still about 120 beats per minute as would be expected. The blood thinners don't 'dissolve' the clot, rather they are an attempt to keep the clot from growing while the body forms a 'cap' of fiber over the clot and shrinks it down over a matter of months. It is not a quick fix.

Later that afternoon I received a page from Mrs. B's nurse. Mrs. B's blood pressure had dropped. Typical blood pressure is 120/80. Mrs. B's blood pressure was 90/40, but she was otherwise asymptomatic. I checked her blood pressure again myself—same reading. Her PE was potentially growing to the point that it was blocking blood flow through the lungs and causing her blood pressure to drop.

IV fluids were started to raise her blood pressure. Mrs. B had to be moved to what is called the 'Step-Down Unit.' Step-Down is a floor for patients that are more unstable than a typical patient in the hospital, but not so unstable that they need to be in the ICU.

Again, nothing happens in the hospital as soon as an intern would like, so it took a couple hours for a room to be cleared in Step-Down and for Mrs. B to be transported. At this point it was about 8 PM in the evening. The nurse checked her blood pressure again— 85/40 and Mrs. B was looking a little 'sleepy' meaning not enough blood was flowing to her brain. We increased the rate of the IV fluids she was receiving, and I told the nurse I would put in an 'art line.' 'Art' is short for 'arterial.'

An art line is like an IV except it goes in an artery instead of a vein and is used to directly and continuously measure blood pressure. Art lines are routinely used in the ICU for patients with hypotension—low blood pressure—which Mrs. B had. Art lines are also more accurate than a blood pressure cuff. Frequently, when the cuff says one pressure, the art line will read a little higher. I was hoping that was the case.

While it was only my third month as an intern, I had already put in 3 art lines during rotations in the Cardiac Intensive Care Unit and the Bone Marrow Transplant Unit. In other words, I 'kinda' knew how to do it. I gathered the supplies, taped Mrs. B's hand over a rolled-up towel so that her wrist was bent back and pointed up. I sterilized her skin with iodine. While the iodine was drying, I set up the art line kit, put on a sterile gown, hair cover, mask with plastic face-shield and sterile gloves.

The art line looks like a long ball-point pen with a needle tip. With one hand you feel for the patient's pulse to locate the radial artery and with the other hand hold the art line like a spear. You insert the art line into where you feel the pulse. You continue pushing it in until you see a flash of bright red blood shoot up about one inch into the clear plastic tube behind the tip—you can even see that blood pulsate.

You then slide a guidewire through the tip and into the artery. Next, you slide a small plastic catheter over the guidewire and slide out the sharp tip. Once you do that, blood starts to come out of the open end of the catheter. You quickly grab the monitor tubing that the nurse has set up next to you and screw the end of the tube onto the catheter. The monitor tubing stops the blood from flowing out and allows the blood pressure to be directly measured on the electronic monitor above the patient's headboard. You then suture the catheter into the patient's skin and cover it with a clear adhesive bandage.

Here is the problem: art lines are typically inserted when a patient's blood pressure is low. If the blood pressure is low, their pulse is very weak so you can barely feel it through your sterile gloves. Sometimes, you can't feel it at all. The radial artery is only a few millimeters wide, so it is easy to miss. I was having this exact problem with Mrs. B.

I could not feel her pulse. Mrs. B's eyes were closed, she was breathing shallowly and her mouth was hanging open. I had seen that look right before a patient was about to code—that's 'hospital-speak' for being on the verge of death. In that emergency situation, the 'Code Blue' team is called to do chest compressions and shock the patient with a defibrillator, if necessary. Mrs. B's heart monitor still showed that she had a pulse of about 120 beats per minute, so I knew her heart was still pumping. I probably should have called a code anyway.

I was having a terrible time trying to get the art line in. I had resorted to blindly stabbing into her wrist with an 'educated guess' as to where her radial artery was. Stab. No red flash of blood. Stab. Nothing. Stab. Nothing. I was getting very hot in my gown. My hand was shaking. I was very nervous.

Then I heard Mrs. B speak, "Sweet Jesus I ask you to help this young man. Sweet Jesus you are good and kind. Sweet Jesus show him strength. Sweet Jesus give him guidance." She continued. I felt emotion well up in me. My eyes teared. I had a hard time seeing. The tears rolled down my nose and dripped onto the plastic face shield of my mask. Mrs. B had spontaneously regained consciousness and was praying for me.

I was not a spiritual person at that point in my life. I did not know where these feelings were coming from inside me.

I got it... a flash of red blood—pulsing, red blood. I slid the guidewire through the tip. It went in smooth and effortlessly. That was a good sign that I had reached the artery. I slid the catheter over the guidewire into the artery, removed the sharp tip, saw the blood come out, stopped the blood with the monitor tubing and screwed it on tight. The nurse synced the monitor. It read 96/42—low, but higher than the last cuff reading of 85/40 and high enough to deliver blood to Mrs. B's brain. I looked over at Mrs. B. Her eyes were closed again.

I finished the art line dressing, tore off my gown and gloves, went to the nurse's station and called the ICU. I told the ICU resident the situation and she said she would be right down to evaluate her for transfer. Meanwhile, the attending physician and senior resident were about to round on Mrs. B. I told them what had happened. They were pleased that I had called the ICU. The ICU resident arrived, went into Mrs. B's room, came out a couple minutes later and said she would take her up to the unit.

While all this was happening, I had been paged several times. My pager went off again. No time to reflect. I had to call them back and keep moving. Mrs. B was now in the hands of the ICU.

I spent the next hour wrapping up some loose ends with other patients and signed out to the on-call intern. I took Mrs. B off my list, which is what you did when your patient went to the ICU.

When I returned to the hospital the next morning, I looked Mrs. B up in the computer to see what had happened overnight. At the top of the screen in bright red letters it read "EXPIRED." I was shocked.

I knew it was early enough in the morning that the ICU resident who had taken her up to the ICU the evening before would still be there. I called the ICU.

The resident told me Mrs. B's blood pressure did not stay up for long and proceeded to go lower and lower. They had had to give her powerful IV medications call vasopressors to make her heart pump harder to keep her blood pressure up. She had to be intubated. Her pressure kept dropping. She coded. They had started chest compressions and gave her more emergency IV mediations to 'jump start' her heart. She had come back, but her pressure started to drop again. They did several rounds of this process—code, compressions, pulse returned, blood pressure up and then down.

Finally, the ICU resident had spoken with Mrs. B's daughter who stayed all night and she decided Mrs. B would not have wanted to continue. The codes were stopped. Mrs. B's pressure dropped again. Her heart stopped. She was gone at about 4 o'clock in the morning. Mrs. B had died from her PE.

Mrs. B was the first patient directly under my care during residency who died. I was totally demoralized. I was so sad for her, for her daughter and selfishly for myself. She had mustered her last strength to pray for me. Her sudden consciousness, my tears, getting her art line in—it all replayed in my mind. I kept staring at the computer screen, mouth open: "EXPIRED."

Lesson Learned:

Human suffering is serious. Death is serious. The term 'healthcare' is somewhat of a glossy euphemism for 'human suffering and death.' Accordingly, the influence of money and business in healthcare is serious.

6

I Can't Read

Mr. D was a man in his mid-70s. He was a widower, but had been remarried for about seven years to Mrs. D. He was a patient of mine in my outpatient clinic at the East Baltimore Medical Center (EBMC), about two miles away from Johns Hopkins Hospital. EBMC was a two story, brick, outpatient facility owned by Johns Hopkins that housed clinics for Internal Medicine, Pediatrics and Ob/Gyn. I saw patients there one afternoon per week.

Mr. D had diabetes requiring insulin, hypertension and congestive heart failure. I saw Mr. D regularly for tweaks in his medication regimen. About half the time he came on his own. The other times he came with his wife.

Mr. D was beyond pleasant: smiling, upbeat and always chuckling about something. Mrs. D was about 20 years younger than Mr. D and was even more pleasant. Mr. D was retired. He worked for 'the railroad,' as he put it, for over 40 years. He had lived in Baltimore his whole life.

I had a hard time getting Mr. D's diabetes and blood pressure under control. His numbers were ok, but not great. A blood test that measures the average level of his blood sugar over the course of 90 days—called a

Hemoglobin A1c test—measured 8.2. The goal is less than seven. Mr. D's blood pressure was consistently around 150/80. The top number—the systolic blood pressure—was too high. The goal for the systolic blood pressure is less than 135 for a person with diabetes.

During one visit, I examined him and we tweaked his medications again. Mrs. D was with him. She had brought me a gift—a plain, black baseball cap that she had bought at the street market just down the hill from Johns Hopkins Hospital. How awesome was that?! It's the first present I had ever received from a patient. I wore it for about three years until it was falling apart.

While I was thanking Mrs. D for the hat, Mr. D interrupted and said "Hey! We gotta go." "Ok," I replied. It was a little unusual for Mr. D to be in a hurry, but I didn't think much of it.

I walked out of the exam room with them. The typical process was to stop by the clerk's desk on the way out to schedule the next appointment. Mr. D said he did not have time for that now and would call later.

"What's the rush?" I asked. "I need to catch the bus to go to school," he replied. "Go to school? Mr. D you're retired. Why are you going to school?" I said almost in a joking manner as I patted him on the back. He continued to walk towards the door.

"I can't read," he said with a smile. He was not embarrassed to say it. I immediately thought about his career at 'the railroad.' "Mr. D, you mean to tell me you worked at the railroad for 40 years and you don't know how to read?" "Yep," he replied.

He put on his own cap that he was holding, shook my hand and walked to the elevator. Mrs. D smiled, shook my hand has well and followed him.

On subsequent visits I came to learn that Mr. D—like so many people who can't read—had created ways over the years to get around his illiteracy. Regarding his medicine, Mrs. D took care of everything for him. She drew up his insulin and then passed him the syringe. She gave him his pills. She did all the cooking and grocery shopping. When it came to Mr. D's diabetes, hypertension and congestive heart failure, Mrs. D ran the show.

No wonder I'd been having difficulty getting his conditions under control. Every time Mr. D came to a visit without Mrs. D, the test results, medication changes and dietary instructions were printed for Mr. D, but he could not read them. He would take them home to Mrs. D and she would do the best she could to follow them without any clarification. I noticed that every time Mrs. D came to the appointments, she always asked tons of questions. I decided Mrs. D had to be there every time. How could I have not picked up on that?

The plan from now on was for Mrs. D to come with Mr. D to his appointments. As expected, Mr. D's numbers improved: Hemoglobin A1c down to 7.5 and his blood pressure down to around 140/80.

Fast forward to near the end of my third and final year of residency, I was on an ICU rotation in the hospital. I had just finished a night of being on call and was headed out of the hospital around 1 PM the next day.

While walking down the hall I ran into one of my fellow senior residents who was on general medicine wards for the month. She told me my clinic patient Mr. D had been admitted several days prior for a CHF exacerbation. He had some excess fluid removed with diuretics and some of his blood pressure medications had been adjusted, too. He was doing well and was set to be discharged in a day.

She added, "He says really nice things about you." I smiled to myself. That was just Mr. D being pleasant as always.

I asked if his wife had been with him. "Yes," the resident said. "What floor is he on?" "Osler 4." That's the name of one of the telemetry floors where patients go with CHF exacerbations.

I went to see Mr. D on my way out of the hospital. He was resting. I touched his shoulder and called his name. He opened his eyes, smiled and reached up to shake my hand. He looked good. It was odd to see him in a hospital gown—he was one of the few patients I was able to keep out of the hospital during my residency. We talked.

It turned out for his birthday, he and his wife went to Atlantic City for the weekend to gamble. They had indulged in several all-you-can-eat buffets. Who could blame him? It was his birthday.

The day after they returned home, he had trouble breathing overnight. He had to sit upright to catch his breath—a classic sign of fluid overload in a CHF exacerbation. The buffet food probably had a lot of sodium, which caused him to retain fluid and led to his shortness-of-breath.

We chatted a little more. He chuckled as always. We said goodbye.

As I left his room, I remembered I should probably tell the senior resident something. I sat down at a computer at the nurse's station. Johns Hopkins had a text paging system, so I could send the resident a message through the computer to her pager as a text.

"Be careful when you discharge Mr. D. He can't read," I typed. I clicked send. I got up and began the 10-minute walk out of the massive hospital and to the parking garage. During the walk I received a text page back from the resident, "Thanks. I had no idea."

Lesson Learned:

High or low 'quality' care is often not a function of money. Patient 'outcomes' are often not a function of money. Quality and outcomes are a function of healthcare professionals effectively interacting with patients and their families. Quality and outcomes are a function of time, attention, understanding and skill repeated over and over again to understand patients' lives. The technical term for this 'understanding of their lives' is called 'social determinants of health.'

Healthcare is a services business. Understanding and addressing those social determinants is a major part of that services business. It's those one-on-one interactions where high quality care and positive outcomes can be found. It is in the interpersonal details.

7

You See, In Afghanistan...

As a resident physician we had many repeat patients. Sometimes we would see the same person every three or four months. Sometimes we would see them every month or even every week. Mr. S was one of those once-a-month patients.

Mr. S was a man in his mid-forties who had also been born and raised in Baltimore. In in teens he began using drugs and became involved in gang activity selling drugs.

Mr. S was well-spoken, ambitious and above all... smart. He was probably one of the sharpest patients I'd ever had. As a result of his characteristics, he rose to become the local leader of his gang and head drug dealer.

I am no expert in gang activity. According to how Mr. S told me his story, his sales and neighborhood territory were growing. Another local gang was not happy about him encroaching on their space. He had several "run-ins" with them. That's how Mr. S described them. I did not know exactly what a 'run-in' was and he did not go into further detail.

However, the disputes came to a head one evening when the rival gang members had pounced on

Mr. S on the street and caught him. They proceeded to take him to a corner telephone booth and had him dial 911. They told him to tell the dispatch operator his location and that he was going to be shot—in the future tense.

At that moment, a rival gang member put a handgun at the base of Mr. S's neck from the back and pulled the trigger. His intent was not to kill Mr. S, but rather he knew that by shooting him in the spine, Mr. S would most likely survive and be a quadriplegic for the rest of his life. He wanted to eliminate Mr. S as competition on the street. Also, he wanted him to suffer a life of disability and send a warning to anyone else who thought about selling drugs in their territory.

As expected, Mr. S survived and was paralyzed from the neck down. Mr. S was down, but not out. He was light on the details, but he had several family members and friends who would feed him, bathe him, change the catheter in his bladder and wipe his bottom after he had a bowel movement. As a drug dealer, Mr. S was also a drug addict. Mr. S's family and friends would also help him shoot up heroin.

Not only did Mr. S continue doing drugs, he continued to work as a drug dealer. His 'people' would come in and out of his bedroom and he would issue directions and orders. He maintained his supply of drugs, divided the money and 'took care' of people when they got out of line. Mr. S had been married and divorced three times.

The years passed. As a quadriplegic, he developed contractures in his arms and legs. Because he was not able to move his extremities, they would become stiff and curled in. Often people who are paralyzed have soft braces that keep their joints in a straight position, so that they do not develop contractures. Mr. S did not have soft braces.

Eventually he had blown out all his veins from shooting up heroin. He had switched over to 'skin popping,' where one injects the heroin just under the skin to form a 'bubble.' The high is not as good as injecting heroin into the veins, so eventually Mr. S switched from skin popping to narcotic pain pills.

Heroin and narcotic pain medication slow down the intestines to the point that they cause mild, then moderate, then severe constipation. Being unable to stand or walk and having to lie in bed all day also leads to constipation. As a result, Mr. S had severe constipation, intestinal blockage and abdominal pain. This pain is what brought Mr. S to the emergency room and to our medical floor.

Mr. S and I did not meet in the hospital until about a dozen years after his gunshot to the neck. He had stopped using and dealing drugs. He said he was too old for that now.

He had been admitted to the hospital for severe constipation and associated gastrointestinal blockage for years. When he became my patient for the first time as an intern, the senior residents and attending physician were already very familiar with him. "Clean him out, Bricker," they ordered. I knew what that meant.

We had to get all the stool out of his colon. As usual, I ordered laxatives and enemas. No results. Mr. S knew this would happen.

"You gotta pull it out," he would say to me every morning on daily rounds. By 'pull out' he meant manual dissimpaction. That is the medical term for putting a glove on and sticking your finger up the patient's rectum to pull out the stool. Mr. S had been manually dissimpacted many times. He knew it was needed to relieve his obstruction.

Given that Mr. S laid in bed all day and no longer sold drugs, he occupied himself by watching CNN and Fox News. My residency at Hopkins was during the height of the wars in Iraq and Afghanistan. Therefore, Mr. S was an expert on international affairs. He loved to talk about it. Interestingly, he was a fan of President George Bush's approach.

The process of manually dissimpacting a person is rather slow. I'll spare you the details, but while I was removing stool from Mr. S's rectum, the T.V. in the room was on and turned to CNN. As usual, the news anchors were discussing the war in Afghanistan.

Mr. S chimed in, "You see in Afghanistan, you've got to get them on their own turf. They mess with you, you gotta let them know that ain't cool and you gotta do to them worse than what they did to you. You see, that's what Bush is doing. He's saying don't mess with us."

He then proceeded to name and easily pronounce the senior leaders of Al Qaeda and the Taliban and what he thought their next move would be. He talked about Guantanamo Bay. He talked about Iraq. He could have written for the journal 'Foreign Affairs.' Apparently, geopolitics is similar to running a gang.

So there I am, hands full of stool learning about world affairs from a constipated, quadriplegic ex-drug dealer.

At the hospital, patients who are admitted often have the insensitive nickname 'frequent flyers.' Mr. S was one of them, but we had many more. Ms. Q was a frequent flyer with sickle cell anemia. Ms. C had chronic obstructive pulmonary disease (COPD).

We even had a 'competition' at the end of each year to see which patient had the most admits. Every year it was the same gentleman—Mr. K. My intern year he had 54 admissions—more than one per week.

Most of the frequent flyers either had no insurance or had Medicaid—which means the hospital most likely was not reimbursed enough to cover the cost of each admission.

Lesson Learned:

Hospitals don't just treat sick people, they are also insurance companies. They take on the financial risk for the health of the community. The ER is always open and has to take anyone.

Many of these patients come back repeatedly and cause the hospital to lose money. Often these people have very unstable social situations. Many are mentally ill. Hopkins did not have a community outreach program to effectively keep them from coming back. Most hospitals don't. They just continue to lose money on their care.

To make up for money-losing patients, hospitals strategize ways to make more money off people with commercial insurance. The industry jargon for this approach is called 'cross-subsidization.' They increase their prices on commercial insurance and charge five to 10 times what they would charge the government under Medicare. They buy imaging centers in upscale suburbs and charge high hospital rates for scans there. They buy physician practices to keep the referrals for tests and procedures coming into their hospital. They advertise 'service lines' on TV commercials and billboards to bring in patients to the money-making areas of their hospital—Orthopedics, Cancer, Cardiology.

None of this is wrong, it just makes healthcare more expensive for people and businesses with commercial health insurance. 'Robbing Peter to Pay Paul' is just how healthcare finance works in America.

8

Have You Ever Seen That Before?

It was my second to last call in the ICU toward the end of my final year of residency. In the past three years I had seen a lot. I had seen a 19-year-old college student with an infected blood clot in her neck and lungs go from being intubated, on a ventilator and having only about a 33 percent chance of living, to walking out of the hospital three weeks later. I had also seen people pass away. High highs and low lows.

In the Hopkins Medical ICU, there were two senior residents who would take call with two interns overnight—one intern for each resident. The two teams of two would alternate taking admissions to the ICU either from the ER, transfers of worsening patients in other parts of the hospital or transfers of ICU patients from community hospitals to Hopkins. My fellow resident had just taken an admit and now I was up.

I received a call from the ER about a new patient. Mr. L was a forty-two year-old male, IV drug user with a fever, elevated white blood cell count, possible pneumonia on chest x-ray and positive blood cultures for bacteria. His blood pressure was in the 100s/60s, tachycardic at 120 beats per minute and he had already received two liters of IV fluid. Antibiotics had been started. The ER had already put in a central-line as well, since they had trouble starting a peripheral IV. His blood pressure had been trending down. He had been in the ER for a while. They wanted to admit to the ICU for sepsis. I said I'd be right down to see him.

He possibly had endocarditis—an infection of the lining of the heart. A person can contract endocarditis from shooting drugs with a dirty needle. Bacteria on the needle travels through the blood stream and attaches to the lining of the heart. From there, it multiplies and 'jumps' back into the blood stream to travel to other parts of the body. If he had pneumonia too, it might be from the same bacteria spreading from his heart to his lungs.

When I saw Mr. L in the ER, he was receiving oxygen through a nasal canula on his face. He was covered with blankets. He was shivering mildly, but otherwise looked relatively comfortable. His eyes were open. He was able to shake my hand and tell me his name—that's a quick test of blood flow to the brain and mental function. If you can shake someone's hand, your brain is working well enough to recognize a social gesture, move your hand and coordinate it so that it reaches the other person's hand. That's a pretty complicated thing to do. It was a good sign.

Mr. L had this already happen several times. After speaking with him, performing a brief exam and reviewing his labs and chest x-ray on the computer, I told the ER resident I would take him in the ICU. He did not look horribly sick, but he seemed to be heading in the wrong direction. Things could get worse before they got better. I went back up to the ICU.

It takes a while, but eventually I saw in the computer that he had been assigned to a bed in the ICU and I could begin entering his admit orders. Nothing happens until the patient gets assigned to you in the computer. I waited some more. He was brought up to the ICU by patient transport and the ER nurse. At this point he had received another liter of IV fluid and he had another bag going in 'wide open.' He was still awake and I quickly told him that the ICU nurse will get him settled in his room and I would come see him shortly after.

The routine is for the ICU nurse to take about 10 minutes to get a new patient hooked up to the monitors, start the admit orders that I had entered into the computer and do their own assessment. His nurse was also in her mid-forties. She only worked nights. Many nurses work either just days or just nights. I had only shared one patient with her before when our shifts had coincided, but I had seen her there many times and knew that she had worked in the Hopkins ICU for a long time.

When she connected Mr. L to the monitors, I could see the results at the nurse's station where I was sitting. His ICU room was about 20 feet away, three rooms down in the corner of the unit so I could not see him from where I was. His heart rate was 125 beats per minute and there was no result for his blood pressure yet. The nurse cycled the blood pressure cuff. It read 90/40. That was too low. Not good.

I go in to see Mr. L and the nurse. Given that his blood pressure was too low, I asked the nurse to put his IV fluids in a pressure bag and start another bag of IV fluids. He was probably going to need vasopressors— powerful IV medications that cause the heart to artificially pump harder to keep the blood pressure up. We were taught to 'fill the tank first' before starting the vasopressors, meaning make sure the patient had enough IV fluids first to make the vasopressor medication as effective as possible.

Mr. L's eyes were still open. He was shivering more. He looked scared. I could hear his muffled voice through the facemask, "I don't feel good." "I'm sorry Mr. L. We're going to give you some more fluid to bring your blood pressure up. It's a little too low right now. That's probably why you're not feeling well." He nodded his head like one would to acknowledge understanding.

"What else do you need?" I asked the nurse. ICU nurses often have additional orders that they need for a patient and I wanted to make sure I put those into the computer too. As soon as I said this, Mr. L began to shake more violently, both arms and both legs. The nurse and I both looked at him. One second later we saw both of his arms start to slowly rise from his side while still shaking. His legs started to rise off the bed too—only about three or four inches, but we could see the blankets rise from his feet underneath. One more second passed. His arms rose higher and higher. They were pointed straight toward the ceiling, still shaking and his back began to arch. It looked like someone was pulling up his body from strings coming down from the ceiling.

Then, "Beeeeeeeeeeeeeeeeeep." It was the well-know and dreaded sound of the monitor when it goes from registering the rapid beep of each heartbeat to the long, constant beep when it can no long pick up heartbeats. The nurse and I instantly locked eyes. "Call a code," I told her. She flipped the blue switch on the wall that activates the code alarm in the ICU.

The rest of the night was a blur. We brought his heartbeat back and he was intubated and put on a ventilator. His heart stopped again. We coded him again. His heart started beating... again. Repeat this cycle about three more times over the course of the night. Amazingly the last time his heart kept beating and stayed beating.

At Mr. L's bedside, the nurse took a few minutes to arrange his IV lines and straighten up the mess of supplies that is typically created during a code. I'm there as well. It was quiet.

I asked her, "Have you ever seen anything like that before?" "What? You mean with his arms?" "Yeah." "No. I've been here for over 10 years and I've never seen that," she finished.

I didn't say this, but it looked like Mr. L's soul was being pulled—or rather ripped—out of his body. He never regained consciousness. Sure, it could have been a seizure from low blood pressure to the brain, but it seemed awfully 'coordinated' and 'purposeful' for just a seizure.

It was about 7 AM. With a lot of people's help we were able to track down Mr. L's sister. She had arrived at the hospital and was in Mr. L's room. She wanted to see him. We talked about what happened and what was going on. I asked her what Mr. L would have wanted in this situation. She replied, "If his heart stops again, let him go." His heart kept beating for about 20 more minutes. Then it stopped. He was gone.

Lesson Learned:

There is something unseen in us. Our bodies are vessels for a Spirit.

The business of healthcare is a business that contends with that Spirit—an unseen Power that we do not fully understand and that we cannot fully control.

9

Spontaneous Applause

Compass Professional Health Services was still in its very early days. We had about a dozen employer clients. The largest client was a housing title company with about 500 employees, but the other companies were less than 100 employees. Our own company had five employees total. As the Chief Medical Officer, I was still responsible for sales, marketing, new client implementation and ongoing account management. All five of us were wearing multiple 'hats' and I certainly was getting a lot of help. I had just sold a new customer—our second largest one. It was a 300-employee water filtration system maker headquartered in Marshall, TX—a small town in East Texas near the Louisiana border.

For new clients, I would explain the Compass 'Personal Healthcare Concierge' service to the employees in person at their employee benefits open enrollment meetings. Open enrollment is typically in the Fall when employees hear about changes to their health insurance, dental insurance and any other benefits they may receive from their employer. Small and mid-sized companies typically have in person open enrollment meetings where their HR department and the various insurance company representatives make presentations on how their coverage works. For example, "Your deductible is 'X.' Your copays are 'Y.'"

These open enrollment meetings are often organized by the company's employee benefits broker— sometimes referred to as an 'insurance broker' or 'benefits consultant.' Most companies have them. They work with the HR department to shop insurance companies to provide the benefits and put them all together in a package. Typically, every year employees must sign up again for their benefits and make any changes such as adding a spouse or children to the coverage.

The water filter company needed to have a 5:30 PM open enrollment meeting for their field sales staff of about 30 employees. The salespeople had flown in from all over the country to attend sales meetings at headquarters. The plan was to have an open enrollment meeting for them at the end of the day and then take them out for a nice steak dinner—as is often done with sales teams. Marshall was about two and a half hours east of our Compass office and my home in the Dallas area.

My plan was to drive that afternoon to Marshall, make my 10-minute presentation explaining the Compass service as part of the overall one-hour open enrollment meeting and drive home that evening after the event was done.

Rather than being at the company headquarters, they decided to have the meeting where they were going to have dinner—a local 'lodge.' As one would imagine, it was a wooden structure with wood paneling on the walls, wood floors and exposed wood beams on the ceiling. There were various stuffed deer and wild hog heads on the walls for decoration. The meeting room had about 15 folding tables arranged in a U-shape with metal folding chairs behind them, facing the font. American and Texas flags stood on top of wooden flag poles in brass stands on either side of the front. It looked exactly like what one would think an East Texas lodge would look like.

The sales staff was about 30 men and one woman—all middle-aged or older. They were dressed casually in jeans, golf shirts and the occasional flannel. About half the men had sausage mustaches and glasses with 1980s-style wire rims. They were laughing and joking around with each other while seated in the folding chairs prior to the start of the meeting.

The company head of HR, Warren, was about 6 foot 4 inches, 280 pounds with greased-back gray hair. With his booming voice he got the sales team's attention and started the meeting. "Hey everybody! Listen up!"

The mood in the room immediately changed. The smiles were gone from the sales team. They stared at Warren, myself, the company's insurance broker and two other insurance company representatives as if we were the mean middle school teacher announcing a pop quiz in class. It was a mix of 'You gotta be kidding me' and 'Here we go again.'

Little did I know that the annual ritual at many company open enrollment meetings involved HR telling the employees that their health insurance deductible was going up and the amount of money coming out of their paycheck was going up. Why? HR would typically say "because the cost of healthcare kept going up and their company had a bad year of claims." Wash, rinse, repeat. Year-after-year. The sales team knew the routine. "How much was the company going to screw us this year," they thought.

I stood to the side by the Texas state flag. I listened to the first speaker—the insurance broker. It was not going well with the crowd. Warren introduced the second speaker—an insurance company representative. Again, not good. Now I'm up.

I began my talk. "Raise your hand if you've ever received a bill from a doctor or hospital?" Every hand goes up. I wanted audience participation to make sure people were awake. At this point in open enrollment meetings, most people are on their cell phones, tuned out and ready to get out of there. "Of course, you have! Silly question. Well, many of those bills are probably wrong," I continued.

I briefly told them about my background as a hospital finance consultant and physician. I explained that Compass was their personal healthcare concierge. Compass would 1) review and resolve their problem medical bills, 2) find doctors that met their specific needs regarding location, availability and clinical expertise, 3) compare prices in advance across doctors and hospitals, 4) help find more affordable medication options and work with their doctor to switch prescriptions, 5) give them price and quality information about specific doctors and hospitals prior to service, 6) schedule appointments, 7) explain how their health insurance works and 8) walk them through their plan choices for open enrollment so they could pick the plan that was right for them.

Compass was not only for their health insurance, but also for their dental and vision insurance as well. Compass was not only for them as employees, but for their families as well.

They had been assigned a dedicated Compass 'Health Pro.' They would receive that Health Pro's name, email address and phone number with direct extension so they could keep working with the same person throughout the year.

Compass did not make medical decisions or 'play doctor.' Compass was their concierge for the administrative complexities of healthcare so that they and their families could focus on getting better and not paperwork. I gave some examples of how employees at other companies used the service.

I finished. There was silence. They were all staring at me. A man at the top right of the 'horseshoe' of tables said in a loud, confident voice, "This is awesome." He began to clap. Everyone in the room immediately followed.

There was spontaneous applause at the open enrollment meeting. I was shocked. I looked at Warren. He was shocked. I looked at the insurance broker—a smile of delight was on his face. He had recommended to

Warren that he hire Compass because he wanted it to have this type of effect on the employees... and it did.

The applause died down. The man who started the clapping continued, "In New Jersey we have the hardest time with this crap. My wife is the one who has to deal with this and she is constantly complaining to me about it. We have two teenagers—their stuff, my wife's stuff, my stuff. It's the worst."

Other salespeople followed with the same types of comments. Salespeople love to talk. The anecdotes started flying. They probably went on for 15 minutes straight. I didn't say a word.

Then the man from New Jersey raised his hand to get everyone's attention. I called on him. "How much does this cost?" He knew nothing was free.

Warren answered for me, "It's free to you. The company is paying for it." The man from New Jersey replied, "Seriously?" "Seriously," Warren answered.

The man from New Jersey clapped, again. Everyone in the room immediately followed, again.

The mood in the room had changed. There were a few more questions for me, which I answered. I passed the floor back to Warren to introduce the next speaker. The positivity of the last 25 minutes had even carried over into the insurance representative's talk. They looked awake and interested as they heard about 'Voluntary Benefits' for accidents, critical illness and cancer.

The meeting ended. Warren vigorously shook my hand. "This better work," he told me. The insurance broker shook my hand. The man from New Jersey came up. He shook my hand and told me a couple quick stories about the trouble his family had been having with bills and doctors. He abruptly concluded with, "Thanks Doc. Now I'm going to go eat steak." He walked off to the dining room.

Compass was on to something. The 'fancy' business term for it is 'product-market fit.' We were starting to see it at Compass. Then it took off... to the tune of 2,000 employer clients.

Fast forward--I personally presented at over 200 open enrollment meetings over the next several years. I did one just off an ocean dock for a salmon fishing fleet in Seattle. I did another in the warehouse of an auto glass company in Fort Worth. There was literally a forklift driving by as I spoke. I've presented at a scrap metal dump that had a junkyard dog—just like you would see in the movies. I've presented to teachers, lawyers, investment bankers, helicopter mechanics, even hospital employees themselves.

We hired more people at Compass to roll out the program. We created an entire implementation and account management department.

Talking face-to-face with Americans of all walks-of-life about their medical bills, doctors and prescription costs has been one of the most rewarding experiences of my professional life. Meeting with HR leaders, CFOs and CEOs about their employees, their health plans and the realities of their operations gave me a front-row seat to business in America.

American businesses are awesome—especially small and medium-sized businesses. They are filled with amazing people who quietly and tirelessly make this country work. It has been a privilege to see their world.

Lesson Learned:

Frequently, healthcare financial problems can be solved with healthcare system navigation. People want it. People need it. The problems are nuanced and particular to the individual, but can be overcome with the help of a healthcare administrative expert.

Healthcare navigation does not lend itself to a scalable, software-only solution. Healthcare is highly services oriented. I'm not sure it can be 'systemically' solved in a generalized way. It has to be personalized.

10

They're Gonna Do This

Compass had moved from a two-room office to a five-room office about six months earlier. It was a stretch. We were only going to take four rooms, but Scott smartly decided to 'splurge' on the lease for a fifth room—a small corner conference room with windows on two sides. The lease was $1,100 a month.

We were in a white, two-story office building in a not-so-safe part of Dallas. We checked the internet map of local crime. There were a lot of car break-ins and theft, but no violent crime. We thought, "That's not too bad." We took what we could afford.

Compass at that time was comprised of three founders and one additional employee. We had about a dozen non-paying customers and four paying customers—the largest of which was the 500 employee title insurance company. We were losing money, but not much, since we only had one employee and a cruddy office. The three founders were taking little-to-no salary.

To save money, we assembled our own Compass brochures. We created a short 'assembly line' of three people: one to assemble the booklet, one to affix the 'glue-dots' and one to stick the wallet cards onto the glue-dots. Repeat. We could do about eight a minute, which is about 500 an hour. We called them 'Packet Parties.'

As the 'sales guy' for Compass, I had been meeting with various insurance brokers and employers for the past two years. Some weeks were slow with no meetings or phone conversations. However, things were slowly gaining steam. I went from no meetings, to some meetings, to some repeat meetings, to a handful of formal proposal requests, to a handful of closed deals. Progress was being made slowly.

Our phones were ringing and the emails were coming in from our members. Our one employee and the three founders worked together to solve every healthcare problem.

One highlight was a bill for $18,000 that a hospital had sent to a member. The bill was in error. His insurance company had already paid, but the hospital felt like it was due more payment. Details aside, we negotiated with the hospital to write off the $18,000 after about three months of work.

The member was a man in his early sixties who was going to retire soon. He had some land out in the country in addition to his home in the suburbs. The land had an old, single-wide trailer on it and he wanted to replace it with a double-wide trailer. It was going to be his retirement home in a couple years. He had delayed the purchase of the double-wide trailer because of the large hospital bill. With the bill gone, he moved ahead with his plans. He was so grateful. It was his dream to live out in the country full time. Obviously, he and his wife weren't 'scraping by' since they had a second home (or trailer, rather), but it was still a big deal to him.

One of the insurance brokers that I had met while attending a local trade association luncheon had a connection at a national retail company. After several phone calls and meetings with this broker, we arranged to have an in-person meeting with the lead benefits consultant for the retailer at our Compass office.

The meeting was five of us: three Compass founders, the insurance broker, John and the benefits consultant, Don. Wanting to make a good first impression, we dressed in suits and ties. John and Don arrived in golf shirts and slacks. I have come to learn this is frequent insurance attire in the South.

John was an enthusiastic believer in our Compass mission to navigate people effectively through the healthcare system and Don was smart and highly inquisitive. We showed John and Don our data and software. Don got so excited, he started laughing. "They've gotta see this!" he said. By 'they,' he meant his retail client.

Two hours later our meeting ended with vigorous handshakes and their promise to speak with the HR and finance people at the retailer about Compass. A week later I received a call from Don. People from the company wanted to come to our office for a visit next month. This company had about 13,000 employees. We had four.

The day of the big meeting came. Our guests from the retailer had flown in for the day from another state. Don was there, too. We had arranged for lunches from a local deli. Our CEO, Scott, picked up the food. We did not want to risk the food being late because of a delivery snag.

We started the meeting and began to learn more about the retailer's particular challenge. The previous year, the retailer had moved to a consumer-directed health plan with a higher deductible and they had seen substantial savings in their medical and pharmacy claims.

However, the employees and management did not like it. There were many complaints. People could not find pricing information about medical services in advance. They were receiving bills from doctors and hospitals that were confusing and seemed wrong. Which ones do they need to pay? Which ones do they need to fight? When they went to the pharmacy, they were being asked to pay hundreds of dollars rather than a $10 copay.

Ironically, a local hospital system had moved all of its employees to a consumer-directed health plan the year before as well. The employees hated it so much that the executives were forced to switch back to the low-deductible PPO plan the very next year and the VP of HR was fired. The retailer did not want either of those things to happen. They had to find a solution and they found it in Compass.

Three hours later the meeting concluded. The senior HR and financial executives helped clear the wrappers and bottles from lunch off the table and threw them in the trash themselves. They did not just leave it. They did not expect it to be done for them. It was a little thing, but it was emblematic of their company culture.

Rather than a large corporation, it was more like a small family company, where everyone pitched in and no job was too small for anyone... including clearing the table after lunch.

I received a call about two weeks later from Don. "They're gonna do this." "You have got to be kidding me!" I said to Don. I didn't mean to. It slipped out. I meant to portray a sense of assuredness rather than shock. Not only was this retailer our first major corporate client, it was a national, household name and would represent enough revenue to pay for the additional employees that we would need to support them.

Fast forward, two months later. We were working on implementation for the group. We had assembled 13,000 Compass brochures... or rather, we had found a way to outsource brochure assembly, which was a much more scalable alternative to our inhouse 'Packet Parties.'

However, we still needed to sort and assemble those brochures into 385 packages for delivery to each of the stores nationwide. By this time, we had three additional employees totaling four Health Pros total, plus the three founders. Scott, Cliff, one of our Health Pros and I were on our hands and knees on the floor stuffing packages with brochures and affixing mailing labels. You can imagine 385 packages spread out across brown office carpeting.

We had also been 'kicked out' of our office space because another tenant was expanding and our lease was month-to-month. On short notice, we found a mildly more presentable building in an only mildly nicer neighborhood with five times the space. Again, Scott was smart to splurge on the amount of space. I thought it was too much. It looked ridiculously empty with only seven people in it, but we ended up needing all the space very quickly.

The packets went out. Within a few days the phones started to ring and the emails started coming in with healthcare requests. We went from 2,000 employee members to 15,000 employee members overnight.

Our first four employees were just the start of a string of amazing hires. They worked hard and fast. They were quick learners, never made any excuses and always had a positive attitude. This was at the depths of the 'Great Recession' and we all knew it was do-or-die: screw this up and we were all out of a job.

Needless to say, it was a success. The employees had a knowledgeable resource to turn to in Compass. Many of their out-of-pocket costs could be reduced and finding the best doctor for the employees often resulted in them not needing expensive tests or procedures.

I continued working on sales. Two months later, I landed a high-level meeting with a national hospitality corporation—another household name. We met. It went well. At the end of the meeting their Director of Benefits asked, "Do you have any major clients similar in size to us that I could talk to?" I smiled. "As a matter of fact..."

Compass' rapid growth began. The next few years were a blur. Meeting. Meeting. Meeting. Sell. Sell. Sell.

Implement. Implement. Implement. Hire. Train.
Support members. Repeat.

Lesson Learned:

Sometimes you need a miracle. There is no reason
a 13,000-employee company should ever use a four-
person vendor. If I were them, I would not have hired us.
But they did. You just have to stick around long enough
for the miracle to happen. To this day, I buy all my suits
from that retailer.

Healthcare improvement in America also needs a
miracle—or rather, many miracles. Some of those
miracles will be big. Most of them will be small, but we
need to keep at it.

11

We Have a Problem

Company C had a problem. Company C is a restaurant chain that sold hamburgers, fries and alcohol. The Great Recession of 2008-2009 had reached its lows and gasoline was $4-$6 per gallon across the country. People stopped going out to eat. The $20 they would have paid for a meal out was now being spent at the pump.

Sales were tumbling. Their stock was in freefall. The layoffs began.

Company C's employee health plan looked a lot like most companies' health plans. They had a Preferred Provider Organization (PPO) plan with a several-hundred-dollar deductible, copays for office visits and prescriptions, and coinsurance—a percent of the medical bill to be paid by the patient—for lab tests, X-rays and MRIs. When all these out-of-pocket costs added up to about $2,000—the out-of-pocket maximum—the health plan would then cover all the costs.

This employee health plan cost Company C about what it cost most other companies—about $10,000 per employee per year and it had been increasing about 7% per year. If any number increases at 7% per year, it will double in about 10 years. At the current pace, their employee health plan would cost $20,000 per employee per year by 2019. The CFO called Company C's Director of Employee Benefits. "We have a problem."

There were multiple ways to lower healthcare costs with one of the newer ones being a 'Consumer-Directed Health Plan' (CDHP). I'll spare you the details, but a CDHP has a higher deductible and no copays for doctor visits or prescription medication. The company gives the employees 'healthcare dollars' on a debit card that they can spend on deductible expenses. Those 'healthcare dollars' would also rollover year-to-year, so the employee could save them for future healthcare needs.

A CDHP ends up lowering healthcare costs by about 5-15% and the annual increase in a CDHP plan is only about half that of a PPO plan. For Company C, that would mean, their health plan costs could go down $1,500 per employee in the first year and in 10 years, would only be about $12,000 per employee per year instead of $20,000 per employee per year.   There are other advantages too: higher rates of preventive care, higher rates of adherence to clinical care guidelines, etc.

However, there are problems with a CDHP. It is not perfect. One problem is that when people have healthcare dollars to spend, they have no idea what anything costs and no idea how to navigate the broken system of doctor, hospital and health insurance billing. It is a disaster. There are other problems too: patients might avoid needed care because they can't afford it and end up sicker, medical bills go to collections and damage people's credit, etc.

Compass was the right service for Company C because Compass allowed them to change their employee health plan from a PPO to a CDHP, while giving their employees and their families a resource to take the billing disaster off their hands. Compass even had an economics PhD from a world-renowned university do a study on the price-per-MRI spending before and after the implementation of the CDHP at Company C. He found that the average cost for an MRI for the company's health plan dropped because employees were going to less expensive facilities for their scans.

The Director of Employee Benefits and her team traveled the country for several years educating the employees about the CDHP. They listened to employee feedback and tweaked the benefit program every year. They also took feedback on the employee experiences from Compass to adjust the program more. They analyzed their medical claims.

The CDHP worked. Company C had lowered their employee health plan costs not by 15%, but almost 30% and their healthcare cost trend had remained below the national level of healthcare inflation. The Director of Employee Benefits at Company C was a hero. Company C had saved so much money on their employee health plan that they did not have to lay off as many people as expected. Reducing healthcare waste was resulting in saving jobs.

The economy recovered. The price of gas went down. People started going back out to eat. With a more cost-effective employee health plan, Company C's earnings grew rapidly and the stock soared—up 600% from 2008 to 2015.

Company C had some executive changes. The CEO retired. The new CEO brought in a new CFO and a new VP of Human Resources. They offered the Director of Employee Benefits early retirement. She left.

The Director of Employee Benefits at Company C had pulled off a miracle. If there was an 'Employee Benefits Hall of Fame,' she would be in it. She was a central reason for the company's recent financial success. She was probably worth 10 times her salary.

Lesson Learned:

The long-term quality and financial performance of an employee health plan is probably only a priority for most corporations when there is a crisis. If you want change, wait for the crisis.

12

We Killed Our Plan

An interesting conundrum takes place with an employee health insurance plan for a healthcare provider itself. One of the relatively early Compass customers was an Ambulatory Surgery Center (ASC). Their insurance broker's name was Ron. Ron was a fantastic individual—real salt of the earth. He had grown up in El Paso driving a WWII era jeep in the mountains that he and his dad had restored together. He looked like a West Texas cowboy—tall, thin, tan skin, with wrinkles of character from the school-of-hard-knocks on his face. Ron had brought Compass on to several other of his clients over the last couple years and their experience had been positive.

Ron called me one afternoon while I was driving from one sales meeting to another. "Dr. Bricker, I've got a problem," he started. "I have a client with about 130 employees that is a surgery center. They are running hot." "Running hot" is health insurance slang for having high medical claims. Before Compass, I didn't even know that health insurance had slang.

According to Ron, there had been six major orthopedic surgeries for employees within the last nine months. The surgeries ranged from arthroscopic knee surgery, to carpal tunnel release, to total knee replacements, to spine surgery. Ron continued, "Go figure. Almost all the doctors who operate at the ASC are orthopedists. You know what they say, 'If you hang out in a barbershop, you're gonna get a haircut.'"

As Ron and I talked more, it turned out he tried to 'shop' the group to various insurance carriers, but no one would offer a quote. Their claims were too high. Their current insurance carrier gave them such a large increase on their renewal for the coming year that it was essentially equivalent to saying 'We don't want your business.'

Now he was stuck with only one insurance company as an option. The ASC was paying about $1 million a year for health insurance coverage, but with their increase they would have to pay $1.4 million. The ASC might have to layoff eight people just to pay for the increase in their health insurance premium.

Ron said he had spoken with the CFO of the ASC and they agreed that they needed to raise the deductible from $500 to $5,000. "What?!" I exclaimed. "I know," Ron answered. "It's the only option we have. And I have to make it an HSA-compatible plan so all the copays are going away too and all the costs less than $5,000 have to be paid by the employees, including prescriptions. It's essentially only catastrophic insurance."

Ron said he convinced the CFO to put in Compass so that the employees had a resource to help them find lower cost medical services and fix any incorrect bills that are sent to them. "I need you, Dr. Bricker, to present Compass to the employees. They are not going to be happy with their insurance change and I need you to show them it's not the end of the world." "Ok. When are the meetings?" I asked.

I arrived on that Tuesday to a two-story ASC that was just down a hill from a large hospital. It was across the street from four fast-food restaurants as well. I met Ron just inside the front door and we took the elevator to the second floor. The ASC was clean, quiet and looked more like a small office building with recessed lighting and various ferns in fancy pots.

We entered what looked to be a training room about the size of two school classrooms. It was already filled with employees—mostly young and middle-aged women in royal blue scrubs. Ron introduced me to the CFO who was there, to his credit. He is the only CFO I have ever seen in an open enrollment meeting to face the employees that his decisions were impacting.

The CFO got everyone's attention and started the meeting. He was straightforward in delivering the bad news about the changes to their health insurance plan. He explained why. He had a kind tone of voice. He expressed regret for what he had to do given all the expensive surgery claims they had over the previous year. There was no blame—more like resignation to fate. He said he was happy to talk to any of the employees anytime in his office.

The employees were silent. The CFO gave the floor to Ron and exited the room. There were a few questions. "Can I still see the same doctor I've been seeing?" "Yes. Your insurance company and network are not changing," Ron answered.

"What will happen when I go to the pharmacy to get my medicine?" "You can still get your medicine, but instead of paying the copay you will have to pay the negotiated rate," Ron said. The woman blankly stared back at him. She had no idea what 'negotiated rate' meant.

The questioning continued for a few more minutes. There was no hostility, just the sense that people were trying to figure out what to do. Ron concluded and introduced me.

I gave my talk. There were more questions. There was some relief in the room around Compass' services.

What I had not said to them was about a dozen of the employees were going to have to pay not just $5,000 more for their healthcare, but really more like $10,000. Like most insurance plans, they still had to pay part of the cost—called the coinsurance—even after the deductible was met, up to $10,000 total. It will be the dozen employees that have significant medical expenses.

The employees would likely need to put the payment on their credit cards at high interest. They would probably feel the financial strain in the form of no vacation and no savings in their kid's college account.

About half the employees would not be affected much at all. They were in good health, didn't take any medications and rarely went to the doctor. For them, they probably just felt bad for the coworkers that had health problems, or more accurately, who's family members had health problems. Some of those employees were well-known. Some were silent.

The meeting ended. There were two more meetings to go. The employees filed out. No chit-chat. Back to work.

There were a few minutes before the next meeting. Ron took me back to the CFO's office. He wanted to introduce us more formally and give him a chance to talk to me.

We walked around two corners and entered a small, windowless office with the overhead lights off and only a desk lamp dimly lighting the room. The CFO was a large man, a little under 6 feet tall and close to 300 pounds. He was probably in his mid-40s.

"Thank you so much for being here, Dr. Bricker," he said, rising from his chair to shake my hand. "I thought you did a good job in there," I responded.

He continued, "We just killed our plan. The employees... they talk with the surgeons. They tell them their problems. The surgeons say they can help. They know they have good insurance since they're employees here. They don't realize that it ends up coming back to bite us. Six major orthopedic surgeries in less than a year?! That's crazy. No insurance company would take us."

Ron added, "When the carrier is calculating rates, they take into account the age and gender of the employees. They also consider the industry of the group.

Healthcare groups always get charged more since they use more healthcare services."

"Do they ever!" the CFO responded. "And since we bill the insurance company through the main hospital's contract, these surgeries are very expensive. We get doubly screwed."

This was more of a nuanced point the CFO was making. There is a movement in America for joint ventures between hospitals and surgery centers. The hospital owns 51% of the ASC and a corporation formed by the surgeons who operate there owns the other 49%.

Because the hospital owns the majority, they get to run the billing for the ASC through the hospital's contracts with commercial insurance carriers. Because the hospital is part of a large hospital system, they have a lot of negotiating power with the insurance carrier. They might demand $16,000 or even $60,000 for a surgery. If they surgery center was independent and had to negotiate with the insurance carrier on its own, they would probably only be able to demand a fraction of that amount.

The hospital and doctors then split the profits 51/49—just like the ownership. As a result, the doctors are not only paid their physician fee for performing the surgery, but also almost half of the facility fee. The physician fee might be several hundred or thousand dollars, but the facility fee can be tens-of-thousands of dollars.

Incorrectly, most doctors and healthcare workers think that they are 'taking' money from the insurance company. In fact, they are not. They are simply taking money from employers.

Most employers with over 100 employees are 'fully credible.' Fully credible means that the employer's premiums are a reflection of their own medical claims. If claims go up, then premiums go up. If claims go down, then premiums go down.

The insurance company aims for 80% of their premiums to be spent on medical claims and they keep 20% for administrative costs and profit. Coincidentally, this 80/20 relationship was the insurance company's goal prior to the Affordable Care Act (ACA) and is now mandated by the ACA. All the ACA did was put that ratio into law. For this surgery center's health insurance plan, all the insurance company did was look at how much they spent in claims for the previous year and add on the 20%.

More claims don't 'hurt' the insurance company. The doctors and hospital are not 'sticking it' to the greedy insurance company. The insurance company is just passing the buck. If anything, the insurance company wants the claims to go up, because 20% of a bigger number means more money for administration and profit.

There you have it. The perfect circle of healthcare costs captured in one employer: a lot of surgeries—some necessary, some probably not-so-necessary, plus high prices negotiated by the hospital, plus an ownership structure that pays the doctors more for doing more, equals higher claims and higher premiums. The surgery center then had to reduce that premium increase by increasing the deductible on the health insurance plan—essentially shifting the cost to the employees.

In this case the creator of the healthcare costs and those feeling the 'pain' of those costs were one in the same. To be more accurate, really it was the doctors and hospital administrators who set up the arrangement who were the 'creators,' and it was the nurses, medical assistants and janitors that felt the 'pain.' To make matters worse, the doctors and hospital administrators were not even on the surgery center's insurance plan, so their deductible did not increase.

Lesson Learned:

There are frequently financial conflicts-of-interest in healthcare. The consequences are real. Anyone who wants to 'make more money' in healthcare has to take it from somewhere. It is a zero-sum game.

13

The Right Doctor

At Compass, one of the main things we did for our employer clients was to help their employees find doctors that met their specific needs. That need might be based on location, availability, or clinical expertise.

One Compass client was a municipality in Florida. One of the employees at the municipality had a daughter—Ms. T—who was on the group's health insurance policy as well. Ms. T needed assistance from Compass.

Ms. T was a 20 year-old student at the local community college. She had a part-time job as well. Unfortunately, Ms. T had been having chronic abdominal pain, nausea and vomiting after eating for the last several years. Her condition had progressively worsened. She had initially gone to the emergency room several times for her symptoms and had been referred to a gastroenterologist—commonly referred to as a 'GI doctor'—for follow up. She had been going to this local GI doctor for over a year. During this time, the doctor had performed an upper endoscopy, colonoscopy and multiple other tests and had diagnosed Ms. T with gastroparesis.

Gastroparesis is a motility disorder of the stomach where the food moves through the stomach and into the small intestines much more slowly than it should. As a result, the stomach becomes 'backed up,' leading to the abdominal pain, nausea and vomiting. It has a broad range of severity, with some cases being so severe that the patient needs to have a permanent tube placed through their skin and into their stomach to allow for the contents to be removed or 'vented' when it backs up.

At first the GI doctor started her on a handful of medications. However, her symptoms only worsened. First, it was more visits to the ER, then it was several hospitalizations. She was in so much pain and discomfort from the vomiting that she eventually had to quit her part-time job and then later had to drop out of junior college.

Her GI doctor tried his best. He repeated the upper endoscopy. He changed some medications. Then he added more medications... and more... and more. Eventually she was on almost 10 medications. After one year, five ER visits and four hospitalizations of over a week each, both she and her family were at wits' end. She was only getting worse and had lost a lot of weight. She was under a doctor's care. She thought she was doing the right thing. Ms. T and her father contacted Compass to see what else they could do.

Gastroparesis is a difficult-to-treat condition within the specialty of gastroenterology. The GI tract stretches from the mouth to the rectum and includes the esophagus, stomach, small intestine and large intestine. This 'tube' is filled with a very complex network of nerves. There are so many nerves that the GI tract has the second highest number of neurons outside the of brain and spinal cord. These nerves allow the GI tract to move food along in wave-like motions called peristalsis. Just like 'catching a wave' at the beach, timing is everything and if the timing of those waves is not coordinated correctly by the electrical impulses of the neurons, then the food does not move forward properly and you can have various problems, including gastroparesis.

Fortunately for Ms. T, there is a branch of the famous Mayo Clinic in Jacksonville, Florida. The main Mayo Clinic hospital and medical school are in Rochester, Minnesota, but Mayo had created a hospital and associated clinics in Florida years ago.

Better yet, Compass had located and connected with the Florida Mayo's dedicated 'Gastroparesis Clinic.' This clinic was staffed by a gastroenterologist, nurses and other staff that specifically diagnosed and treated gastroparesis—not heartburn, not stomach ulcers, not colon polyps—just gastroparesis.

The Gastroparesis Clinic also had pain management specialists, psychiatrists, counselors and a support group. Because the GI tract has so many nerves, stress and emotions must be addressed. Additionally, the Gastroparesis Clinic had an intensive three-week outpatient program where all the specialists would meet with the patients.

Ms. T and her father made the four-hour drive to Mayo, had the initial appointment and were enrolled in the three-week outpatient program. Details aside, by the end of the three weeks, Ms. T had gone from almost 10 medications to two and her symptoms had dramatically improved. She was gaining weight and better able to function. She returned home.

Several months later our Compass Health Pro, Emily—who had assisted Ms. T and her father—traveled to the municipality for their employee benefits vendor 'fair.' Sometimes these events are called 'Wellness Fairs' or 'Employee Health Conferences.' It is an opportunity for employees to learn more about the services that are available to them—from medical and dental insurance to their 401K retirement plan.

Emily stood at her booth, like all the other vendors, except she was greeted by a joyful hug from the father of Ms. T. He told Emily the rest of the story: When Ms. T returned home, she eventually was able to re-enroll in school. After trying that out and having it go well with her gastroparesis, she returned to her part-time job. She was happy, smiling and able to live a life she had not lived in several years. Ms. T's recovery had a positive impact on her whole family. Ms. T's father said the Mayo Clinic in Jacksonville had saved them all.

When Emily told me this whole story, I could not contain myself—I was so excited. We had seen firsthand the power of connecting a patient in need 1) with the right doctor, 2) with the right expertise, 3) with the right team, 4) with the right intensity and frequency of visits. That's how the magic happens. That's how healthcare 'gets solved.'

Lesson Learned:

There is a real 'mismatch' problem in healthcare. Patients and diseases are highly variable. Some diseases are easy—e.g. strep throat. Some diseases are hard—e.g. gastroparesis. Doctor skill is also highly variable. Some doctors and medical teams are a little skilled in a lot of things. Some are more skilled in a few things. Some are very skilled in only one thing. Some are not very skilled in anything.

The key to high quality diagnosis and treatment is to have the easy diseases treated by the medical teams that have a little skill in a lot of things. If the disease is more complicated, the patient needs to be referred to a specialist, rapidly. If the disease is too complicated for that specialist, the patient needs to be referred to a sub-specialist, rapidly. This 'escalation' of the patient to the right doctor, with the right expertise, at the right time requires competence and humility on the part of the doctor and the right financial incentives. In today's world, the doctor 'loses' money when they refer the patient to someone else.

Solving the 'mismatch' problem won't fix everything, but healthcare quality and cost problems probably will not be solved until patients are referred correctly. The great news is... it is a solvable problem.

14

We'd Like To Visit with You

Compass had been growing like a rocket. We had over 700 employer clients including multiple major national corporations and even several universities. We were selling our services all over Texas and across much of the country. Almost every insurance broker and benefit consultant in the Dallas – Fort Worth Area introduced Compass' services to their clients. The insurance carriers were starting to take notice.

That's when I received the email. The VP of Marketing for one of the major insurance carriers wrote, "We'd like to visit with you." Fantastic, I thought. I rushed to tell our CEO Scott. I figured they had seen the value of our service. They had seen the impact Compass was having on their members and their employer clients. Surely, they wanted to partner with us and distribute our service to more of their client-base.

How naive of me. I could not have been more wrong.

Scott and I visited their office about two weeks later. It was a massive, 16-story, new building. It had a huge lobby that stretched the entire first floor from front-to-back. I was amazed that it was totally open with no support columns. It looked like an indoor football field with a low ceiling. It was covered with cream-colored stone on the floors and walls.

We registered with security and received our badges. An executive assistant greeted us and walked us to a bank of elevators. We took an elevator to the top floor.

When the doors opened, it was clearly the executive offices. There were no boring, gray cubicles. Even the largest, multi-billion-dollar corporations I had seen had boring, gray cubicles. Nope. This office had all deep, stained wood desks separated by stained wood partitions, with individual offices along the outside with glass walls. There were a lot of brass lamps. It seemed odd to see lamps in an office—usually there is just the fluorescent, overhead lighting.

She led us to a corner meeting room with an oval conference table with about 10 chairs around it: four on each side and one at each end. We were the first ones in the room. She said she was going to tell the others we had arrived. She left.

Then the VP of Marketing entered. I had no idea what the VP of Marketing looked like, but he immediately said his name, so I knew he was the gentleman who had emailed me. Next entered a rather short, older gentleman, a middle-aged woman and two more men in gray suits. The older gentleman sat at the head of the table, the VP of Marketing to one side and the woman to the other. The two gray-suited men sat at the other end of the table. Scott and I sat on the same side in the middle.

We all shook hands. The older gentleman said he was the President. The woman said she was in operations. The two gray-suited men were from the central office in another city. They had flown in for the meeting. Again, naively I thought it was going to be just me, Scott and the VP of Marketing.

He started the meeting. "We've been hearing a lot about Compass in the market. We'd like to hear more from you about what you are doing?" Scott and I looked at each other. I nodded at Scott to have him take the lead if he liked. He began.

The questions from everyone in the room started only after Scott had been speaking for about 30 seconds. Ninety minutes later the questions and answers stopped. "Well, this has been very interesting," the President said. The VP of Marketing continued, "These two gentlemen from the head office are in Product. We really think of ourselves as 'Fast Followers.' We are going to build a service that is similar to Compass. Thank you for coming."

They stood. We stood. We shook hands. No one said anything. It was awkward.

We walked out of the meeting room. The executive assistant was there. The VP of Marketing said she would show us out. She walked us to the elevators and pushed the down button. We waited. Again, no one talked. We entered the elevator and descend to the lobby. We walked to security at the entrance. The executive assistant said, "I need to have your badges back now."

We handed them to her. "Thank you for coming," she said. We walked out.

Within about six months the insurance carrier launched their copycat service to their existing customers. Some of those customers were already Compass customers, too. They offered their service at a price about 30% less than ours. For their larger customers—and our larger customers too—they offered it for free. We kept most of our customers, but we lost some to the insurance carrier's free service.

For employers that used this insurance carrier, but were not yet Compass customers, our future sales slowed... dramatically. They wanted something cheap that was already baked-in to one of their existing vendors, so they didn't have to deal with anybody else.

Regardless of any differences or perceived differences in quality or value between the two services, Compass had something the insurance carriers would never have: we were not them. In general, people do not like and do not trust insurance companies. The service and the people providing the service at the insurance carrier might be great, but the employees at their members tend to not want to interact with them. Even if they do, they don't necessarily follow along with what the insurance carrier is saying.

Compass adjusted. Rather than engage in a race-to-the-bottom on pricing with their new service, we refocused on different markets and employers that had different insurance carriers. Two years later, another insurance company did the exact same thing. A year after that, another and a year after that, another still.

Of course, the price of the service from the insurance carrier was not really 'free.' They could just 'bake' the price into their other fees and premiums that they were already charging the employers. The insurance carriers were doing to us what Microsoft Word did to Word Perfect in the 1990s—they created a me-too product for desktop publishing that could be sold as a part of their software 'platform' and box out the competition.

Lesson Learned: Almost any start-up in healthcare will be viewed as a threat to incumbents. It's only natural. I was dumb not to expect it. Those incumbents have a choice: buy or build. They will either buy the healthcare start-up and bring it into their fold or they will build a competing product or service and squash the competition.

If I had learned my history better, I would have known that this is exactly what Rockefeller, Carnegie and Vanderbilt did. As Mark Twain said, "History doesn't exactly repeat itself, but it rhymes."

Change in healthcare is tough. A lot of people don't want it, or if they do want it, they want it on their terms.

15

Paid for Compass for the Next 50 Years

I entered the elevator on the first floor of a nondescript 12-story office building in a fancy part of the city. I pushed the "12" button in the elevator. The top floor was the 'family office' of one of the oldest and wealthiest families in the city. The family office was a Compass client.

Before this group was one of our clients, I had no idea what a 'family office' was... some sort of company that made custom offices in people's houses, I incorrectly thought. A family office is where rich people put their money and assets so that when they die, they can keep it in the family. This family office was also the holding company of multiple large businesses.

The offices were nice, but not extravagant. Everything was white. Many of the rooms had glass walls, so you could look across most of the floor from office to office.

I checked in with the receptionist. I was led through a maze of glass walls and hallways to one of the meeting rooms in the middle of all the glass. In the room were the two insurance brokers for the family office. Soon after I walked in, the VP of HR and Director of Benefits walked in as well.

The purpose of the meeting was to review their group's utilization of the Compass service during the previous year and talk about new Compass features for the coming year. I had brought utilization reports to discuss and a presentation of what was new at Compass.

The family office holding company had about 50 employees and the plan was to try the Compass service out with this group first before introducing it to the larger companies that the holding company owned.

Over the course of the meeting we reviewed the case of one employee who needed to have prostate surgery. His urologist had initially scheduled the employee's surgery at Oak Tree Medical Center. As he had known from working with Compass for other healthcare services, he wanted to see a review of the hospital's quality and price information. He had a consumer-directed health plan with a high deductible. His company did put a large sum of money in the employee's Health Savings Account every year to pay for deductible expenses. He contacted his Compass Health Pro.

Compass was very familiar with Oak Tree Medical Center. It was a new hospital in the area that was out-of-network with all insurance carriers. It did not even take any Medicare patients. However, the surgeons that operated there were in-network with most insurance carriers. The surgeons at Oak Tree also operated at other area hospitals including one just five miles down the highway.

As a result of being out-of-network, Oak Tree's prices were very high. They performed orthopedic, urologic, gynecologic and bariatric (weight-loss) surgery for tens-of-thousands or even over $100,000 more than other in-network hospitals. The doctors would tell the patients that they themselves were in-network and would be able to see them for their pre-operative evaluations. However, when it came time for surgery, the surgeon would schedule them at the out-of-network Oak Tree Medical Center.

This arrangement is expensive for patients and their employer-sponsored insurance plan. Most people have separate in-network and out-of-network deductibles on their health insurance plans. Even if the patient had reached their deductible as part of their pre-operative visits, scans and tests, they would have to start from zero for the hospital cost for their surgery because they had not met any of their separate out-of-network deductible yet.

This employee's prostate surgery was going to cost about $75,000 at Oak Tree. That exact same surgery with the exact same surgeon at the in-network hospital just five miles down the road would cost only $25,000. Given that the less expensive hospital was also in-network, it would result in a dramatically less overall out-of-pocket cost for him as well—to the tune of thousands of dollars.

His Compass Health Pro notified him of the price difference and asked if he wanted Compass to look into other hospital options for him with his same urologist. As one could imagine, he was interested.

Compass contacted the urologist's office and after speaking with the office manager and the urologist's nurse, the employee's surgery was rescheduled for a different day at the $25,000 in-network hospital down the road. The employee had the surgery done and recovered well without incident.

As it was later revealed in a law enforcement investigation and in the local newspaper, Oak Tree Medical Center was incentivizing surgeons to perform operations at their expensive out-of-network hospital by paying for marketing—such as billboards and advertisements—for the surgeons and even paying the salaries of employees that worked in the surgeons' offices. These 'perks' were essentially kickbacks and it is against the law for hospitals to provide kickbacks to doctors for referring patients to their facility. As a result, one or several of the administrators for Oat Tree Medical Center ended up in prison and the hospital closed.

This 'bait-and-switch' approach with an in-network doctor and an out-of-network facility was well known by Compass. Compass had also seen this approached used at other hospitals, ambulatory surgery centers and endoscopy centers across the country. This 'scam' would result in $20,000 out-of-network colonoscopies performed by in-network gastroenterologists. Typically, the facility charge for an in-network colonoscopy is only $800-$1,200.

As we concluded discussing this employee's experience with Compass, the VP of HR said that she had talked about this same story with the group's CFO, who then replied, "With what we saved, we just paid for Compass for the next 50 years." We all laughed. Sadly, scams and complicity of doctors in those scams are not funny at all.

Lesson Learned: Caveat Emptor—Buyer Beware. That saying holds true in most consumer situations and to a certain extent that is to be expected. However, healthcare is unique in that it is often an infrequent service, at a stressful time, that is filled with fear and uncertainty. Add to this mix a doctor who has superior knowledge and is providing guidance. Most people have learned to trust doctors since they were children. Those factors create a perfect storm for potential abuse and exploitation.

16

Target, a Pathfinder and a New Place

One of the most amazing things about Compass was the opportunities it created for our employees. When I started Compass with Scott and Cliff, I never imagined that giving people a job could be so rewarding. I just wanted to help people in their health and healthcare. I had no desire to be a source of income or livelihood for people. That was probably just a short-sighted thought on my part.

As previously mentioned, Compass started gaining traction and hiring employees at the bottom of the 'Great Recession' in 2009. For a recent college graduate, it was a terrible time. Many people were unemployed or taking jobs that did not require a college degree. Many recent graduates moved back in with their families. In some respects, their adulthood was being delayed.

Our second employee, Julia, had grown up in the area and lived at home while going to a local four-year college. She had graduated with good grades only to take a job as a check-out clerk at Target. Never one to complain, she appreciated having any job even though it did not pay enough for her to move out and rent an apartment of her own.

Being very bright, her job at Target did not challenge her mentally the way she could be challenged. She had tremendous talent in organizational skills, interpersonal communication and creative problem solving. She made an ideal Health Pro and the Compass position was perfect for further developing those amazing skills that she had. There is certainly nothing wrong with working at Target. However, she had the ability to grow professionally and apply her talents to helping people who had complicated problems navigating their healthcare and health insurance.

During her time at Compass, one of the members that Julia was assisting died. We would some Compass members pass away over the years. When people are sick with cancer or heart disease, they don't always recover. Julia had been working with him and his wife for several months on bills, prescriptions and coordinating care towards the end of his life.

After he passed away, the bills kept coming. If you die, the doctors and hospitals still expect payment. The member's widow kept communicating with Julia who kept working on the bills for months. Eventually all of the bills stopped coming and Julia had finished determining which bills were correct and needed payment by insurance, which needed payment by the widow and which needed to be removed because they were incorrect.

A week later, Julia received an email from the Head of HR at the company where the member had worked. The Head of HR had received an email from the widow expressing her gratitude for the Compass service and more importantly Julia. The Head of HR had never received an email like this and not only did she forward on the widow's email to Julia, but she added her own appreciation as well.

If my memory serves me right, Julia did not bring the email to my attention. She was too modest to show off her great work. However, she had shared the nice note with one of her coworkers to show the impact they were having on peoples' lives. It was this coworker who brought the email to my attention.

Wow! Amazing! Julia was the perfect person, in the perfect place, at the perfect time to help this man, his widow and the employer. Years after this event, Julia and I would still reminisce about it.

Like Julia, Ray was a recent college graduate from a large state school and was living at home. Ray drove a Nissan Pathfinder from the 1990s. It was about 13 years old and it was a gas guzzler.

Ray had a special knack with people when they were upset. He always remained calm, showed tremendous empathy and was able to 'cool them off' so they could rationally describe the healthcare problem they were having. When people are dealing with medical bills and prescription costs, their emotions tend to run high. There is a sense of unfairness. Many people are angry... angry at their insurance company, angry at the hospital, even sometimes angry at their doctor.

Because Ray was so good with people when they were upset, we assigned Ray to those members that had health insurance policies with the most out-of-pocket costs. These members received the most bills and tended to be irate. These members would usually call rather than email their questions. Since they were so upset, they needed someone to vent. They would vent to Ray.

Eventually, almost a year went by and I was chatting with Ray at his cubicle, which was tucked away in a back corner. Ray was excited to tell me that he had just bought a 'new' used car. He finally was able to afford to get rid of the gas-guzzling Pathfinder and he had bought a 'pre-owned' Volkswagen Jetta. It was as if Ray had won the lottery, he was so happy. I was happy for him.

I think part of the reason Ray was so happy was that his Pathfinder was so run-down that it was embarrassing to drive. He was dating a young woman and I think he was self-conscious about his vehicle. Maybe I'm reading too much into it, but to work, provide value, get paid and then take that money and use it for an improvement in your life feels good. It's incredibly satisfying. I could see that satisfaction on Ray's face.

Stacy was yet another recent graduate from a major Texas university. She too had not been working since graduation and was living at home with her parents and sixth grade sister. Stacy was Health Pro number four at Compass and was hired at almost the same time as Julia.

She was assigned as one of the main Health Pros for the 13,000-employee retail client and she knocked it out of the park. I would have client phone calls with the retailer's HR executives, and they would say that employees were singing praises about Stacy by name.

Stacy and I had even developed a program where we would have three-way calls with her, the member and myself to go over more complex medical issues related to conditions like multiple sclerosis, Crohn's Disease or cancer. I would not give medical advice, but together, Stacy and I would devise a strategy for the member to get to the right type of doctor with the right expertise and communicate that plan to the member.

Like Ray, one day Stacy came 'bouncing' into work. I was in the small kitchen of our office pouring coffee when we ran into each other. "What's going on?" I asked.

"I just got an apartment!" Stacy replied. "Wow!" Stacy continued to explain that she had been looking at places for several weeks and finally decided on a brand-new apartment building in a suburb of Dallas—on the other side of town from her parents. I'm sure that was just a coincidence. "It's so cute. It's a one bedroom. I can't wait to decorate it."

Selfishly, I felt great that Stacy felt so great. She had worked toward a goal of moving out of her parent's house. She had saved up for it for over a year. She was moving out and she was thrilled.

Many of our other Compass employees had worked for us for several years and then gone on to careers as account managers at insurance brokerages and benefit consulting firms. Others became managers in HR at corporations or administrators at hospitals and insurance carriers. Some went on to law school or medical school. Our employees were getting married, having children and buying homes of their own. It was the best thing ever to watch.

Lesson Learned:

Helping people navigate their healthcare and health insurance is a great driver of job-creation. The value derived from making the healthcare experience smoother, higher quality and lower cost for patients can be translated into a meaningful income, which can allow people to achieve their goals in life. Business can be an amazing thing.

Summary of 16 Lessons in the Business of Healing

1. Doctoring is a pyramid: 'fighter-pilot' specialists are on the top and 'infantry' primary care physicians are on the bottom.

    Implication: Changes in physician payment will affect the different specialties differently. Doctors are not a monolith.

2. Ill thoughts and ill families lead to ill bodies.

    Implication: Spending more money on ill bodies may not lead to health if a person still has ill thoughts and families.

3. Physicians who teach medical students sacrifice income to train the next generation of doctors.

    Implication: Current pressure to maximize physician revenue today may lead to decreased instruction and expertise of future doctors.

4. The US labor market for physicians, nurses and other healthcare providers depends on foreign-born and foreign-trained people.

    Implication: Immigrants are a vital part of the US healthcare system.

5. Money in healthcare has life and death consequences.

   Implication: The good and bad sides of capitalism are starkly juxtaposed in healthcare.

6. Educational and social circumstances unique to the individual have a major impact on a person's disease and its treatment. This uniqueness in healthcare is a makes the standardization of 'mass production' and 'scale' difficult to apply.

   Implication: Effective healthcare is patient-specific. Protocols can still be used, but they must take into account the realities of a patient's circumstances.

7. Hospitals take on risk, just like insurance companies.

   Implication: The insurance industry is regulated in terms of the amount of reserves each company must have. The concept of 'regulated reserves' could be applied to hospitals as well to control their current 'Robinhood' approach of overcharging commercial insurance to compensate for Medicare and Medicaid underpayment.

8. The metaphysical world dominates the physical world.

   Implication: In healthcare, maybe our physical money challenges have metaphysical solutions.

9. Healthcare system navigation is a key component to solving healthcare financial challenges—both for individuals and employers.

    Implication: Historically, doctors and hospitals themselves have not provided the adequate services to navigate patients through their own system. Likewise, insurance carriers have not provided the needed navigation services either. Employer-led healthcare navigation is a way to fill that gap.

10. In order for healthcare entrepreneurs and startups to succeed, they need employers to take on the risk of using their service.

    Implication: The perpetual high cost for employer-sponsored healthcare and health insurance could be due in part to the risk-averse nature of employers in this area of their operations.

11. Employers tend to make substantial changes in employee healthcare only when there is a crisis.

    Implication: A lack of change in employee healthcare and their health insurance vendors is to be expected in the absence of a crisis.

12. There are financial conflicts-of-interest in healthcare that are often hidden.

    Implication: Reducing conflicts-of-interest may be a key component to improving healthcare.

13. Many of the problems of healthcare quality and cost can be solved by matching a patient with the right doctor and team of providers at the right time.

    Implication: There are 'pockets of greatness' within the US healthcare system. The key is to get the right people to those pockets at the right time.

14. Change in healthcare will be resisted by those people and organizations that benefit from the current system.

    Implication: Any calls for change by those people and organizations that already benefit from the current US healthcare system should be met with skepticism.

15. The intermittent and emotionally-charged nature of healthcare makes patients especially susceptible to exploitation.

    Implication: One of the values of an advocate in healthcare is their greater frequency and rationality with healthcare situations.

16. Improving quality and cost-effectiveness in healthcare creates value that can be translated into income for businesses and people.

    Implication: The future of a career in healthcare is bright if you can create real benefit to others.

Epilog

To learn more about healthcare finance, I have started a video journal called AHealthcareZ.

It can be found at AHealthcareZ.com

The journal has over 100 videos, each about four to seven minutes in length.

Topics range from hospital/insurance contracting to pharmacy benefit managers to case studies of employers that have successfully increased healthcare quality and decreased healthcare costs.

You can subscribe to the AHealthcareZ Video Newsletter via a link on the homepage.

Made in the USA
Monee, IL
11 June 2020